Coretta Scott King Award Books

DISCUSSION GUIDE

Coretta Scott King Award Books DISCUSSION GUIDE

Pathways to Democracy

by Adelaide Poniatowski Phelps *and* Carole J. McCollough

Office for Literacy and Outreach Services and ALA Editions

An imprint of the American Library Association
Chicago | 2014

Printed in the United States of America

18 17 16 15 14   5 4 3 2 1

Extensive effort has gone into ensuring the reliability of the information in this book; however, the publisher makes no warranty, express or implied, with respect to the material contained herein.

ISBN: 978-0-8389-3604-7 (paper).

Library of Congress Cataloging-in-Publication Data

Phelps, Adelaide Poniatowski.
   Coretta Scott King Award books discussion guide : pathways to democracy / Adelaide Poniatowski Phelps and Carole J. McCollough.
     pages   cm
   Includes bibliographical references and index.
   ISBN 978-0-8389-3604-7 (alk. paper)
   1. Coretta Scott King Award—Bibliography. 2. Democracy—Study and teaching (Elementary). 3. Democracy—Study and teaching (Secondary). 4. American literature—African American authors—Bibliography. 5. American literature—African American authors—Study and teaching. 6. Children's literature, American—Bibliography. 7. Children's literature, American—Study and teaching. 8. Young adult literature, American—Bibliography. 9. Young adult literature, American—Study and teaching.
   I. McCollough, Carole J. II. Title.
Z1037.A2P46 2014
016.8108'0928208996073—dc23   2013043085

Book design by Kim Thornton in the Chaparral and Caecilia typefaces.
Cover illustration © KathyGold/Shutterstock, Inc.
Background photo © nagib/Shutterstock, Inc.

♾ This paper meets the requirements of ANSI/NISO Z39.48-1992 (Permanence of Paper).

Contents

CHAPTER 2   ## Grades 2–4 47

CHAPTER 3   ## Grades 3–6 63

CHAPTER 4   Grades 4–8 103

CHAPTER 5   Grades 6–10 139

CHAPTER 6 **Grades 7–12** **175**

CHAPTER 7 **Grades 9–12** 235

Foreword

> The function of education is to teach one to think intensively and to think critically . . . Intelligence plus character—that is the goal of true education.
>
> —*Martin Luther King, Jr., 1947*

DEMOCRACY AND ITS CORE VALUES HAVE MORPHED OVER the centuries just as the function of education has evolved. My personal educational philosophy is situated in the Head Start movement of the late 1960s, in itself a movement toward democratic values. I was a college student, soon to become a teacher. My introduction to the program was a week's training on working with Appalachian children. Although the vast majority of children we served were African American, there was no training aimed at working with them.

Over the next few years, I learned little about diversity and equality—or inequality, for that matter. Martin Luther King, Jr. was assassinated, Bobby Kennedy was killed, Vietnam raged on, and education trudged on. In some U.S. cities, changes appeared gradually, but we only have to examine the inequality in post-Katrina New Orleans to see that the core values of democracy continue to be suppressed in much of American education.

How do we expect the situation to improve? One effective strategy that can achieve permanent change is to allow children to explore, study, understand, and eventually integrate the democratic values into their everyday lives. To do this, children must be exposed at home and at school; values must be taught, encouraged, and modeled on a daily basis. What are the core democratic values that enable children to mature into responsible citizens? As the authors of this book explain, core democratic values include *a dynamic sense of community, history, and social responsibility.*

Martin Buber (as cited in Guccione, 2011) distinguishes between objectifying students as data—scores on a test—and creating a relationship between students and teachers or teachers and administrators. His "I-it" and "I-thou" philosophy can illuminate the ideals contained in the core democratic values. Buber advocates teachers who establish relationships with students as colearners, viewing each student as a person who has value and can bring worthwhile skills and knowledge to each learning experience. Current educational journals and blogs are abuzz with articles and opinions about the Common Core State Standards (CCSS). When we standardize all curriculum, we objectify students—whether preschool or postgraduate—as we might sort widgets. The assumption is that all students learn the same way at the same speed and will perform equally on standardized tests. This philosophy does not value the individual student, nor does it recognize the cultural knowledge and skills students bring to the classroom. It is the opposite of Buber's ideals.

I do not mean that improving curriculum and learning expectations is wrong. The theory behind the CCSS is solid. However, as we say, the devil is in the details. Unless teachers and administrators understand how to integrate the core democratic values into the Common Core State Standards, we will continue to graduate students who know little about their duties and responsibilities as citizens of the world.

What are core democratic values? A democratic core curriculum "involves not only common knowledge but also the values and processes of the democratic way of life" (Beane, 2002, p. 27). According to Beane, this involves integrating self-interest and the common good, valuing diversity, asking powerful questions, and doing real work. If all of these occur, students will meet the rigorous standards that are called for in the CCSS and will "learn to respect one another, contribute to the group, and build a community in the classroom" (Beane, 2002, p. 28).

Depending on the age and level of education, the explanation of essential democratic values can be simplified or expanded. Most of these values come directly from the U.S. Constitution, its amendments, and the Bill of Rights. Themes include the following core democratic values:

- **Equality**—everyone has an opportunity to achieve.
- **Pursuit of happiness**—individuals can pursue happiness without impeding others' quest for happiness.
- **Rule of law**—people show obedience and respect for authority.
- **The common good**—cooperation so that all people can succeed.
- **The right to life**—inviolable except in extreme cases defined by law.

Adelaide Phelps and Carole McCollough have provided a road map to help teachers and librarians incorporate values lessons into read-aloud sessions or book club discussions. They include focal and supplemental books that are suited for young children up to high school seniors. Both Phelps and McCollough have served on the Coretta Scott King Book Awards jury, with McCollough having also served as its chair. Their meticulous reading of Coretta Scott King Award books, as well as Pura Belpré, Newbery, Caldecott, and other Association for Library Service to Children (ALSC) award-winning books offers librarians and teachers a treasury of discussion topics, books, and questions that will challenge readers to think deeply and broadly about their responsibility as a citizen.

John Dewey, one of the twentieth century's greatest proponents of education for democratic values, wrote:

> All the aims and values which are desirable in education are themselves moral. Discipline, natural development, culture, social efficiency are moral traits—marks of a person who is a worthy member of that society which it is the business of education to further. (John Dewey, 1916)

Linda M. Pavonetti, EdD
Oakland University, Rochester, MI
Vice-President, International Board on Books for Young People

REFERENCES

Beane, J. A. (2002). "Beyond Self-Interest: A Democratic Core Curriculum." *Educational Leadership* 59 (7): 25–28.

Boydston, J. A., ed. (1976). *John Dewey: The Middle Works: 1899–1924. Vol. 9, 1916: Democracy and Education.* Carbondale, IL: Southern Illinois University Press.

Guccione, L. M. (2011). "The Tale of Two Schools." *Schools: Studies in Education* 8 (2): 252–264.

King, Jr., M. L. (1947). "The Purpose of Education." [Published in *The Maroon Tiger,* Morehouse College, Atlanta, student newspaper]. Retrieved from www.drmartinlutherkingjr.com/thepurposeof education.htm.

Acknowledgments

W E GRATEFULLY ACKNOWLEDGE OAKLAND UNI-
versity's Educational Resources Lab (ERL)
in Rochester, Michigan, and the Southfield
Public Library in Southfield, Michigan, for
providing space for research and access to
their collections. An extra word of thanks
goes to Barbara Jones Clark, Birmingham Public Schools in Birmingham, Michigan. We are particularly grateful to Barbara Begin Campbell,
coordinator of the ERL, for providing us access to her support staff,
especially Karen Reeves, circulation manager, and Edith Tanniru and
Julie Chapie, technical support. We specifically wish to thank the American Library Association for its continuing support of the Coretta Scott
King Book Awards.

Introduction

OUR GOAL FOR THIS BOOK WAS TO TAKE THE DISCUSSION guides created by the Coretta Scott King (CSK) Book Awards jury for each year's award and expand this resource to create a handbook useful to educators, librarians, parents, and other child caregivers. We did not include every Coretta Scott King Award book. We reviewed every winner, honor, and John Steptoe title and evaluated them based on appropriateness as they relate to the core democratic values, rather than by subject or theme. We chose core democratic values as a way to frame these discussions, using a Socratic approach, assuming the understanding that rules are essential for avoiding total chaos. The interpretation of rules depends on the perspective of those affected by the rules. Coretta Scott King Award books provide a venue for discussing pathways toward a better understanding of what these rules and their accompanying responsibilities mean.

We embarked on a search to identify within the plot, character, and themes of CSK-winning titles those values that relate to being an American citizen in a democratic society. It soon became clear that most if not all of the CSK titles embodied the responsible decision making that is integral to living in a constitutional democracy. The decision was made to use the Socratic method of discussion to highlight core democratic values. Our hope is to expand the utility of this body of literature by and about African Americans to a broader audience for a deeper purpose.

In a democratic society, responsibility plays an important role. So, if we focus on the core democratic value of pursuit of happiness, for example, trust and truth telling are important aspects of that pursuit. For children in K–4, *Storm in the Night* by Mary Stolz, illustrated by Pat Cummings, offers opportunities to discuss these aspects of the pursuit of happiness.

If we think broadly about the pursuit of happiness and look at the various ways that teens pursue this happiness, Alice Childress's *Rainbow Jordan* offers many opportunities for discussion. Compare it with Sharon Draper's *Forged by Fire, Tears of a Tiger*, or Virginia Hamilton's *Sweet Whispers, Brother Rush*. View the same titles with a focus on right to life, and the perspective will be entirely different. This makes the Coretta Scott King Award books essential to discussions about developing a strong sense of citizenship.

Core democratic values inform our discussions of CSK titles. They complement the theme of a book while not necessarily relating specifically to the subject area of the book. They are basic to both American and global perspectives and include the foundations and values of life in a democratic society. CSK authors speak from a variety of perspectives. Respect for others, responsibility, citizenship, honesty, trustworthiness, community awareness, and fairness: these are the underlying principles of American society. They are expressed in the Declaration of Independence, the United States Constitution, and the Bill of Rights. They embody fundamental beliefs in life, liberty, pursuit of happiness, common good, justice, equality, diversity, truth, popular sovereignty, and patriotism, along with the constitutional principles of rule of law, separation of powers, representative government, checks and balances, individual rights, freedom of religion, federalism, and civilian control of the military.

Life in a democratic society is heavily laced with responsible decision making. Coretta Scott King books present multiple opportunities to explore aspects of core democratic values as themes. CSK books expand the limited view about African American lives with a depth not previously explored, thereby moving our thinking toward what it means to live in a democratic society. This includes privileges, responsibilities, and a dynamic sense of community and history.

As we examined each individual title, we determined that several CSK titles from the 1970s and 1980s were either not available or were inappropriate for our stated purposes. We looked at the themes and the complementary core democratic values and developed "Content Perspectives" that reflect these values. "Discussion Openers" focus on a particular aspect of the title as a starting point.

"Beyond the Book" addresses the 'thinking piece' or starting point for understanding how youth literature provides pathways to successful living through a better understanding of universal values. CSK Award books can help youth readers work through daily issues and concerns while inviting them to view the larger picture of living in a democratic society.

In "Books for Further Discussions," we selected books again based on appropriateness as they related to the core democratic values, including Newbery, Caldecott, Pura Belpre, Sibert, Schneider, Jane Addams, and American Indian Award books, as well as books that did not win an award. This approach allowed us to remain focused on a pathway toward discussions about what it means to be a good citizen.

We started this project with a focus on core democratic values. We took titles from each award year and determined if, how, and where the core democratic values applied. Coretta Scott King Award books emphasize these values. What it means to be a citizen in a democratic society is at the core of this project. We see this effort as an opportunity to open discussions about important aspects of citizenship—both privileges and responsibilities—that are often overlooked. This includes a dynamic sense of community, history, and social responsibility. We want to move Coretta Scott King Award books from the limited view of celebrating African American life into the broader perspective of daily democratic living and into the global realm.

CHAPTER 1

Grades K–3

The Bat Boy & His Violin

By Gavin Curtis,
illus. by E. B. Lewis
N.Y., Simon & Schuster, 1998
Grade: K–3
Genre: Fiction/Picture Book
Core Democratic Value: Liberty
*Follow your beliefs and let
others follow theirs.*

Content Perspective

Reginald wants to practice his violin for an upcoming recital in church.
His dad, who happens to be the manager of the Negro League team the
Dukes, insists that he travel with the team as a bat boy. Watercolor paintings by E. B. Lewis bring a perspective that combines the two diverse
story elements of sports masculinity and musical sensitivity. Reginald
manages to continue his pursuit of musical excellence while at the same
time awakening an unexpected music appreciation from the team players.

Discussion Openers

Students should provide examples of text and/or illustrations to support their responses.

- Look at each of the pictures of Reginald playing the violin. Notice that his eyes are closed. Why do you suppose that is?
- Why is it important to Reginald that his father not call his violin a fiddle?
- Find the picture of the Dukes in front of the bus. How do you know what the men were thinking or feeling?
- Talk about the way Papa thinks about Reginald playing the violin. Describe how Papa's feelings changed.
- How did Reginald respond to his father's love of baseball?
- How did the players respond to Reginald's music?

Beyond the Book

- Ask an elder in your family if he or she can tell you anything about the Negro Baseball League.
- Retell the story, emphasizing the key details.
- Ask your teacher to help you find a Schubert sonata; listen to it with your classmates.
- What special skill or talent would you like to have?
- In this story, all of the characters got what they wanted: Reginald's father got his son to become a bat boy; the players got a new musical awareness; Reginald got to practice for his upcoming recital. How did that happen?

Books for Further Discussions

- *Catching the Moon: The Story of a Young Girl's Baseball Dream* by Crystal Hubbard, illus. by Randy DuBurke. Lee & Low, 2005.
- *Mighty Jackie: The Strike Out Queen* by Marissa Moss, illus. by C. F. Payne. Simon & Schuster, 2004.
- *Violet's Music* by Angela Johnson, illus. by Laura Huliska-Beith. Dial, 2004.
- *What Charlie Heard* by Mordicai Gerstein. Farrar, Straus and Giroux, 2002.

Beautiful Blackbird

By Ashley Bryan

N.Y., Atheneum, 2003

Grade: K–3

Genre: Folktale/Picture Book

Core Democratic Value: Diversity

Work and play with everyone.

Content Perspective

Ringdove and all the forest birds pro-
claim Blackbird the most beautiful
of them all. In keeping with Ringdove's request, Blackbird adorns his
fellow birds with touches of his blackening brew. His task complete,
Blackbird advises, "Color on the outside is not what's on the inside . . .
Whatever I do, I'll be me and you'll be you." Ashley Bryan's message of
self-acceptance and tolerance—and the often repeated "Black is beautiful. Uh-huh!"—emphasizes that beauty comes from within.

Discussion Openers

Students should provide examples of text and/or illustrations to support
their responses.

- Beautiful Blackbird shared some of his color with all of the other
  birds. How did it make the other birds feel? How did it make Beauti-
  ful Blackbird feel?
- What did Beautiful Blackbird mean when he said: "Just remember,
  whatever I do, I'll be me and you'll be you"?
- Why did the other birds think that Blackbird was the most beautiful
  of all?
- What made Beautiful Blackbird a good friend to all the other birds?
- Reread the last page and discuss how the birds felt about Beautiful
  Blackbird for sharing his color.

Beyond the Book

- How can sharing contribute to happiness?
- When you share something how does it make you feel?
- How would you respond if someone asked you to share your lunch? Would you respond differently if they asked you to share your candy?
- Using colorful paper, create your own collage of birds and tell their story.
- Go on a nature hike and describe all the birds that you see and hear.

Books for Further Discussions

Brown Honey in Broomwheat Tea by Joyce Carol Thomas, illus. by Floyd Cooper. HarperCollins, 1993. (CSK Honor)

Just in Case by Yuyi Morales. Roaring Brook, 2008. (Pura Belpre Winner/Honor)

My Family Plays Music by Judy Cox, illus. by Elbrite Brown. Holiday House, 2003. (CSK–John Steptoe Winner)

The Patchwork Quilt by Valerie Flournoy, illus. by Jerry Pinkney. Dial, 1985. (CSK Winner)

Uncle Jed's Barbershop by Margaree King Mitchell, illus. by James Ransome. Simon & Schuster, 1993. (CSK Honor)

Black Cat

By Christopher Myers
N.Y., Scholastic, 1999
Grade: K–3
Genre: Fiction/Picture Book
Core Democratic Value: Diversity
Work and play with everyone.

Content Perspective

Black Cat roams the New York landscape paying homage to the diverse environment of commercial and residential structures, playgrounds, street trash, subway rodents, and basketball courts. *Black Cat* is creatively illustrated with a unique combination of cut paper, photographs, paint, and random found street items. It celebrates the variety experienced in city neighborhoods.

Discussion Openers

Students should provide examples of text and/or illustrations to support their responses.

- Compare Black Cat's neighborhood to your own. What is the same? What is different?
- Which places did Black Cat go that seemed the most dangerous? Why? Are there places in your neighborhood that might be dangerous?
- Which places did Black Cat visit that seemed the most exciting? Why?
- Find five new or unfamiliar words and look up their dictionary meanings.
- Answer the questions, "Where is your home; where do you go?"
- Explain what is meant by "throwing shadows and tags on graffiti-covered walls."

Beyond the Book

- Discuss how the fabled nine lives might be useful to Black Cat.
- Give the book a new title and explain why you chose it.
- Create a map of your neighborhood. Add a key that shows the location of your school and other important buildings.
- Black Cat traveled alone. Who might his friends have been?
- Black Cat was at home wherever he went. What does home mean to you?

Books for Further Discussions

Looking Like Me by Walter Dean Myers, illus. by Christopher Myers. Egmont, 2009.

Me and Uncle Romie: A Story Inspired by the Life and Art of Romare Bearden by Claire Hartfield, illus. by Jerome Lagarrigue. Dial, 2002.

Tar Beach by Faith Ringgold. Crown/Random House, 1991. (CSK Winner, Caldecott Honor)

Uptown by Bryan Collier. Henry Holt, 2000. (CSK Winner)

The Blacker the Berry

By Joyce Carol Thomas,
illus. by Floyd Cooper
N.Y., HarperCollins/Amistad, 2008
Grade: K–3
Genre: Poetry
Core Democratic Value: Diversity
Work and play with everyone.

Content Perspective

Twelve free verse poems celebrate and affirm the varied skin tones of African American children. Poem titles reflect the visual vocabulary of Joyce Carol Thomas. The thematic motif of bread and berries throughout support the characteristics of diversity: "Biscuit Brown," "Snowberries," "Raspberry Black," and "Toast." Floyd Cooper illustrates thoughtful, self-assured, and spirited children in the poems.

Discussion Openers

Students should provide examples of text and/or illustrations to support their responses.

- Look at the faces of the children in the book and describe the expressions or moods of the children.
- "The blacker the berry" is the first part of a common saying among African Americans. The remaining part is "the sweeter the juice." Why do people say it?
- Look at the illustration for "Sunshine Girl." Notice the colors in the art and the way Cooper uses light to draw your eye around the page. Read the poem on the page aloud. How did Cooper use the words to inspire his art?
- In "Snowberries," Thomas mentions the *one drop rule*. Think about the reason for such a rule. Ask a significant adult in your life to explain the meaning of that rule.
- How would you describe your skin using words from Thomas's poems?

Beyond the Book

- Copy one of the shorter poems. Underline the adjectives and circle the nouns. How do the adjectives add to or change the poem?
- Reread and discuss with classmates the poem "What Shade Is Human?" Then write your own poem about the color of human.
- Look at your face in a mirror. Describe your skin tones using words from Thomas's works.
- Find a poem and divide the lines up with a friend. Perform for your classmates.
- Share three things you know about blackberries.

Books for Further Discussions

All the Colors of the Race by Arnold Adoff, illus. by John Steptoe. Lothrop, Lee and Shepherd, 1982. (CSK Honor)

Black Is Brown Is Tan by Arnold Adoff, illus. by Emily Arnold McCully. HarperCollins, 2002.

Brown Honey in Broomwheat Tea, by Joyce Carol Thomas, illus. by Floyd Cooper. HarperCollins, 1993. (CSK Honor)

Skin Again by bell hooks, illus. by Chris Raschka. Hyperion/Jump at the Sun, 2004.

Dave the Potter: Artist, Poet, Slave

By Laban Carrick Hill,
illus. by Bryan Collier
N.Y., Little, Brown, 2010

Grade: K–3

Genre: Nonfiction

Core Democratic Value: Liberty

Follow your beliefs and let others follow theirs.

Content Perspective

Dave the Potter was an enslaved person living in South Carolina during the 1800s before and after emancipation. No record of his birth or death exists. Evidence of his life resides in the pottery he created, a stark reminder that people are more than what they appear to be. Dave was no ordinary artist. He worked with huge slabs of clay that were excavated and "ground in the pug mill and carried, / wheelbarrow after wheelbarrow, / to Dave's spinning potter's wheel." Sometimes he turned out pottery big enough to hold a man. Sometimes he put words on his pots, "Dave belongs to Mr. Miles / wher the oven bakes & the pot biles." Step by step, Laban Carrick Hill walks us through the process Dave used in creating his unique pottery. Bryan Collier's exquisite illustrations use warm earth tones that extend the story and provide a glimpse into what Dave the Potter's life might have been like.

Discussion Openers

Students should provide examples of text and/or illustrations to support their responses.

- Look at the illustrations and provide evidence of Dave the Potter's strength.
- Consider the illustrations and discuss Dave's talent as an artist.
- Look at the illustration of the two enslaved men hauling wheelbarrow after wheelbarrow of clay to Dave's potter's wheel. Tell the story

of these two men. How might their lives have been different from Dave's, and how might they have been the same?

- How did Dave express his ideas about family, friends, and slavery? Explain what your examples mean.
- What kind of freedom did Dave have? How does it compare to the freedom that you have?
- What was most important in Dave's life?

Beyond the Book

- Write a story about a talent that you have, and illustrate it.
- Imagine that you are Dave the Potter. What two lines would you write on your pottery that would let people that you will never meet know what kind of person you are?
- What kind of community would we have if American citizens did not have the freedom to learn to read and write?
- Write a story about what you thought Dave the Potter's life was like. What did he do when he wasn't making pottery?
- Dave the Potter had very strong hands. Trace an outline of your hand and write on it all the things you can do with your hands.

Books for Further Discussions

Freedom River by Doreen Rappaport, illus. by Bryan Collier. Hyperion/Jump at the Sun, 2000. (CSK Honor)

Harvesting Hope: The Story of Cesar Chavez by Kathleen Krull, illus. by Yuyi Morales. Harcourt, 2003. (Pura Belpre Honor, Woodson Honor, Jane Addams Winner)

Moses: When Harriet Tubman Led Her People to Freedom by Carole Boston Weatherford, illus. by Kadir Nelson. Hyperion/Jump at the Sun, 2006. (CSK Winner, Caldecott Honor)

When Harriet Met Sojourner by Catherine Clinton, illus. by Shane W. Evans. HarperCollins/Amistad, 2007.

An Enchanted Hair Tale

By Alexis De Veaux,
illus. by Cheryl Hanna
N.Y., Harper & Row, 1987
Grade: K–3
Genre: Fiction
Core Democratic Value: Equality
Give everyone an equal chance.

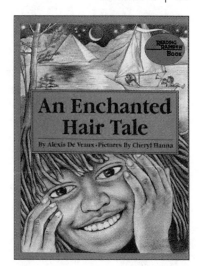

Content Perspective

Sudan is just a little boy who lived once in time. He has his father's eyes, his father's lips, and wild mysterious hair like his mother. It is his hair that troubles him the most—a "fandangle" of hair that sometimes sprouts wings and that sometimes draws ridicule from grown-ups. When Sudan discovers the circus in town, he encounters people that look more like him, friends of his mother, and begins to see just how he fits into his neighborhood, hair and all.

Discussion Openers

Students should provide examples of text and/or illustrations to support their responses.

- Why did grown-ups make fun of Sudan's hair? What effect did that have on Sudan?
- Do you think it was right for grown-ups to make fun of Sudan's hair? Why or why not?
- Toward the end of the story, what did Sudan see when he looked in the mirror? How did it make him feel?
- How did Sudan's mother feel when Sudan left home?
- This story is a fantasy. What makes it so?

Beyond the Book

- Look at the picture on page 40 and compare it with an illustration from Maurice Sendak's *Where the Wild Things Are*.
- Create a list of action words from *An Enchanted Hair Tale* and write sentences using the list.
- How is the word *blue* used on page 14? What does it mean within the context of the story?
- De Veaux uses metaphorical language to describe Sudan's hair on page 24. Look in a mirror and describe yourself using similar language.
- Has anyone ever made fun of your hair? How did it make you feel?
- Have you ever made fun of someone else's hair? How did that make you feel?

Books for Further Discussions

The Ant Bully by John Nickle. Scholastic, 1999.

Bird Child by Nan Forler, illus. by Francois Thisdale. Tundra, 2009.

Dave the Potter: Artist, Poet, Slave by Laban Carrick Hill, illus. by Bryan Collier. Little, Brown, 2010. (CSK Winner, Caldecott Honor, Woodson Honor)

Martin's Big Words: The Life of Dr. Martin Luther King, Jr. by Doreen Rappaport, illus. by Bryan Collier. Hyperion/Jump at the Sun, 2002. (CSK Honor, Jane Addams Winner, Orbis Pictus Honor, Caldecott Honor)

Goin' Someplace Special

By Patricia C. McKissack,
illus. by Jerry Pinkney
N.Y., Atheneum, 2001
Grade: K–3
Genre: Fiction/Picture Book
Core Democratic Value: Equality
Give everyone an equal chance.

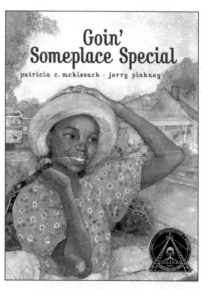

Content Perspective

Tricia makes her first trip to the public library alone. The 1950s segregated South means she must sit in the "colored" section of the bus. She also is not allowed to sit on park benches marked FOR WHITES ONLY when she walks through the park to look at the beautiful fountain her grandfather helped to build. Getting swept into a hotel by a crowd following a celebrity changes the meaning of someplace special for Tricia until she is reminded by neighbor "Blooming Mary" of her beloved grandmother's words: "You are somebody, a human being—no better, no worse than anybody else in the world."

Discussion Openers

Students should provide examples of text and/or illustrations to support their responses.

- What message did 'Tricia recall from Mama Frances about the signs on the bus?
- Make a list of the encouraging words 'Tricia heard from different people she met as she made her way to someplace special.
- What evidence do you have that 'Tricia had good manners?
- Describe 'Tricia's thoughts and feelings when she makes it to her destination.
- Discuss three reasons why it was important that 'Tricia could read.

Beyond the Book

- Did anyone in the book do something you did not like? Describe the action and explain why it offended you.
- What did the title have to do with the book?
- Pretend you are recommending this book to a classmate. What would you say?
- What surprised you about the story?
- Where are you allowed to go without an adult?

Books for Further Discussions

Rosa by Nikki Giovanni, illus. by Bryan Collier. Henry Holt, 2005. (CSK Winner, Caldecott Honor)

A Sweet Smell of Roses by Angela Johnson, illus. by Eric Velasquez. Simon & Schuster, 2005.

This Is the Dream by Diane Z. Shore and Jessica Alexander, illus. by James Ransome. HarperCollins, 2006.

Jazzy Miz Mozetta

By Brenda C. Roberts,
illus. by Frank Morrison
N.Y., Farrar, Straus and Giroux,
2004

Grade: K–3

Genre: Contemporary Realistic
Fiction/Picture Book

Core Democratic Value: Equality
Give everyone an equal chance.

Content Perspective

Miz Mozetta wanted to dance. All she needed was some dance companions. Dressed in her fanciful duds, she heads out the door. Her friends are full of aches, pains, and excuses; "Not me, Miz Mozetta. My dancin' days are done, honey dear." Disappointed but not discouraged, she sashays across the street where young people are dancing all the newest moves. When she realizes they just want her to sit and watch, she sadly returns to her home and flicks on the radio. Before long there is a knock on the door, and all her old friends have changed their minds. As they begin to jitterbug the night away, the young kids from across the street hear the music and decide to join the party, determined to learn the "new" jitterbug moves. Frank Morrison's illustrations jump off the page as he makes the characters come alive.

Discussion Openers

Students should provide examples of text and/or illustrations to support their responses.

- How can you tell that this particular evening was important to Miz Mozetta?
- What did Cap and Rudy think when Miz Mozetta asked if she could join their dance?

- What did Miz Mozetta think when Rudy and Cap told her to sit and watch while they danced? How did it make her feel?
- What caused Rudy and Cap to change their mind about Miz Mozetta?
- Select your favorite illustration and discuss how lines and color are used to help tell the story.

Beyond the Book

- Identify a "Jazzy Miz Mozetta" in your life. Explain your choice.
- Have you ever been excluded from an activity that you really wanted to join? How did it make you feel?
- Have you ever deliberately excluded someone from an activity? How did that make you feel?
- What can you find out about the jitterbug from the adults in your family?
- Using the picture book, *H.O.R.S.E.*, illustrated by Christopher Myers, compare Myers's illustrative style with that of Morrison in *Jazzy Miz Mozetta*.

Books for Further Discussions

Emily's Eighteen Aunts by Curtis Parkinson, illus. by Andrea Wayne von Köngislöw. Stoddart Kids, 2002.

Jazz on a Saturday Night by Leo and Diane Dillon. Blue Sky, 2007. (CSK Honor)

Neeny Coming, Neeny Going by Karen English, illus. by Synthia Saint James. BridgeWater, 1996. (CSK Honor)

The Patchwork Quilt by Valerie Flournoy, illus. by Jerry Pinkney. Dial, 1985. (CSK Winner)

Storm in the Night by Mary Stolz, illus. by Pat Cummings. Harper & Row, 1988. (CSK Honor)

Uncle Jed's Barbershop by Margaree King Mitchell, illus. by James Ransome. Simon & Schuster, 1993. (CSK Honor)

Mirandy and Brother Wind

By Patricia C. McKissack,
illus. by Jerry Pinkney
N.Y., Knopf, 1988

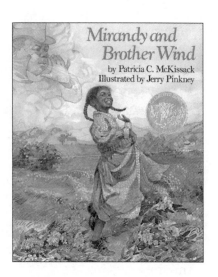

Grade: K–3

Genre: Fiction/Picture Book

Core Democratic Value:
Pursuit of Happiness
All people can find happiness in their own way, as long as they do not step on the rights of others.

Content Perspective

Beautiful illustrations complement the colorful language of the old South in this story of cakewalks and Mirandy's effort to win by capturing the power of Brother Wind. Mirandy enlists family, friends, and neighbors in her preparation for the Ridge community grown-up and junior cakewalks. A special wish and a surprise partner help Mirandy "take the cake."

Discussion Openers

Students should provide examples of text and/or illustrations to support their responses.

- Do you think it was a good idea for Mirandy to try to capture the wind? Why or why not?
- What is meant by *conjuring*? What clues are given by the text?
- What information is provided by the illustrations and what information is provided by the author's words?
- Describe what is happening in the first illustration of the story.
- Choose a character in the story and describe how their actions contribute to Mirandy's pursuit of happiness.

- Retell the story, including specific details about characters and major events.
- Can you explain what might have happened when Ezel asked Orlinda to be his partner?
- Choose one of the adults in the story. Describe how that person helped or hindered Mirandy.

Beyond the Book

- Investigate online the history of cakewalks. Share your findings with your classmates.
- What happened next? Share with your classmates a continuation of the story.
- Imagine that Brother Wind was Sister Wind. What difference, if any, would that make to the story?
- Make a list from your reading of female characters that exhibit strong, self-determined characteristics.
- Read *Uncle Jed's Barbershop* by Margaree Mitchell. Write a description of the rural South using picture and/or text details. Can you name other books that take place in the rural South?

Books for Further Discussions

Bat Boy & His Violin by Gavin Curtis, illus. by E. B. Lewis. Simon & Schuster, 1998. (CSK Honor)

Jazz on a Saturday Night by Leo and Diane Dillon. Blue Sky, 2007. (CSK Honor)

Jazzy Miz Mozetta by Brenda C. Roberts, illus. by Frank Morrison. Farrar, Straus and Giroux, 2004. (CSK–John Steptoe Winner)

The Piano Man by Debbi Chocolate, illus. by Eric Velasquez. Walker, 1998. (CSK–John Steptoe Winner)

My Family Plays Music

By Judy Cox,
illus. by Elbrite Brown
N.Y., Holiday House, 2003
Grade: K–3
Genre: Fiction/Picture Book
Core Democratic Value: Diversity
Work and play with everyone.

Content Perspective

This talented family loves all manner of music: marching band, country, classical, jazz, organ, and every kind of music you can think of. So it's only natural that the storyteller finds a way to participate musically with each member of her family. The festive mood of the illustrations invites an appreciation of every musical genre.

Discussion Openers

Students should provide examples of text and/or illustrations to support their responses.

- Look at the glossary at the end of the book. There are many types of music. Music for a sing-along, music for dancing, and music just for listening. Which type do you prefer? Why?
- Does anyone in your family play music? What instrument? Can you find that instrument in the book?
- Look at the clothing worn by different musicians. How is what the musicians wear related to the music they play?
- Select an illustration and retell what is happening.
- How many instruments can you identify in the story?

Beyond the Book

- Look at the list of instruments the girl in the story plays when she accompanies different members of her family. Which ones are familiar to you?
- Locate recordings of three types of music. Share them with your classmates.
- Do you know anyone who plays a musical instrument professionally? Talk to them about the type of music they play. Share your conversation with your classmates.
- Create your own simple musical instruments. What music can you make with them?
- Trace the origins of various musical instruments. Which ones can be traced to Africa?

Books for Further Discussions

Dizzy by Jonah Winter, illus. by Sean Qualls. Arthur A. Levine, 2006.

Ellington Was Not a Street by Ntozake Shange, illus. by Kadir Nelson. Simon & Schuster, 2004. (CSK Winner)

Jazz by Walter Dean Myers, illus. by Christopher Myers. Holiday House, 2006. (CSK Honor)

Jazz on a Saturday Night by Leo and Diane Dillon. Blue Sky, 2007. (CSK Honor)

The Piano Man by Debbi Chocolate, illus. by Eric Velasquez. Walker, 1998. (CSK–John Steptoe Winner)

My Rows and Piles of Coins

By Tololwa M. Mollel,
illus. by E. B. Lewis
N.Y., Clarion, 1999
Grade: K–3
Genre: Fiction Picture Book
Core Democratic Value: Common good
Help others.

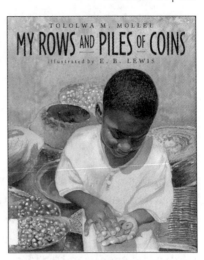

Content Perspective

Saruni regularly goes to the market with his mother, Yeyo, to help with market work. There are many tempting goods to buy with the coins he earns. Saruni resists spending on treats, taking his coins home to a secret money box. Saruni has his eye on a bicycle that he will use to carry goods to and from the market for his mother. Saruni watches his stash of coins grow as he separates them, lines them up, and counts them each week. Finally, when his pile of coins grows to 305, Saruni feels he must be the richest boy in the world. He packs the coins in bundles and sets off to market to buy a bicycle to help his mother with market work.

Discussion Openers

Students should provide examples of text and/or illustrations to support their responses.

- Look at the picture of Saruni going to market with his mother. What was in the wheelbarrow? How easy or hard do you think it was to push the wheelbarrow?
- Sometimes other people laughed at Saruni. How do you think that made him feel?
- Saruni wanted a bicycle to help make the market work easier for his mother. Talk about ways he showed responsibility for the grown-ups in his life.

- Think about a loaded bicycle. How did Saruni solve the problem of riding a bicycle loaded with market goods?
- Choose an illustration from the book. Ask and answer a question about it.

Beyond the Book

- Using the "Author's Note" at the end of the story, calculate how many American coins it would take to make 150 Tanzanian shillings.
- Do you know how to ride a two-wheel bicycle? What was the most difficult part of learning?
- Have you ever been to a farmers market? How is the farmers market in your city the same or different from the one pictured in the book?
- Would you be willing to save money for something an adult in your life needed? Why or why not?
- The people in the story walked to the market each week carrying their goods in baskets. Where do you walk? If you have something to carry, how do you carry it?

Books for Further Discussions

Do I Need It or Do I Want It?: Making Budget Choices by Jennifer S. Larson. Lerner, 2010.

I Can Make a Difference by Marian Wright Edelman, illus. by Barry Moser. HarperCollins, 2005.

Less Than Zero by Stuart J. Murphy, illus. by Frank Remkiewicz. Harper-Collins, 2003.

Neeny Coming, Neeny Going by Karen English, illus. by Synthia Saint James. BridgeWater, 1996. (CSK Honor)

Neeny Coming, Neeny Going

By Karen English,
illus. by Synthia Saint James
Mahwah, N.J., BridgeWater,
1996

Grade: K–3
Genre: Historical Fiction/
Picture Book
Core Democratic Value:
Common Good
Help others at home and school.

Content Perspective

Essie can't wait for cousin Neeny to return to her small island off the coast of South Carolina. Neeny left to go live with her mother in the big city on the mainland. City life changed Neeny in ways that Essie finds uncomfortable. Can Essie find a way to anchor Neeny's heart to her home island? In spite of Neeny's resistance, a last-minute surprise connects her forever to the island that Essie still calls home.

Discussion Openers

Students should provide examples of text and/or illustrations to support their responses.

- When Neeny returned to the island, she had changed. What were the effects of living in the city?
- Do you think it was right for Neeny to stay in bed when Essie had planned things for them to do in the morning?
- What ideas justify Neeny leaving the island?
- Was everyone on the island happy to see Neeny? Why or why not?
- How did Neeny feel about people on the island?
- How did people on the island feel about Neeny?

Beyond the Book

- Neeny changed after living on the mainland. How has your life changed during the last year?
- Explore the Gullah culture of South Carolina online. Share three things that you learned.
- Imagine that you are Neeny and you just arrived home in the big city. How would you feel when you opened Essie's package?
- Imagine that you have to leave home and move to a new place. Talk about what that might feel like.
- Sit with a new classmate at lunch and ask them where they came from and what it feels like to be in a new school.

Books for Further Discussions

Back Home by Gloria Jean Pinkney, illus. by Jerry Pinkney. Dial, 1992.

Bring Me Some Apples and I'll Make You a Pie: A Story About Edna Lewis by Robbin Gourley. Clarion, 2009.

The Chicken-Chasing Queen of Lamar County by Janice N. Harrington, illus. by Shelley Jackson. Farrar, Straus and Giroux, 2007.

Sweet Potato Pie by Kathleen D. Lindsey, illus. by Charlotte Riley-Webb. Lee & Low, 2003.

Uncle Jed's Barbershop by Margaree King Mitchell, illus. by James Ransome. Scholastic, 1993. (CSK Honor)

Night on Neighborhood Street

By Eloise Greenfield,
illus. by Jan Spivey Gilchrist
N.Y., Dial, 1991

Grade: 1–3

Genre: Poetry

Core Democratic Value:
Pursuit of Happiness
*Have fun but follow the rules at home
and school.*

Content Perspective

A poetic celebration of community spirit, cohesion, and challenges are experienced by Juma, Tanya, Darnell, Nerissa, Karen, and Lawanda, all residents of Neighborhood Street. Illustrations reflect joyful play, bedtime ritual, extended family gatherings, and spiritual support for the demands of keeping a family healthy and safe.

Discussion Openers

Students should provide examples of text and/or illustrations to support their responses.

- What do you know about the neighborhood from the picture of children playing sidewalk games at dusk?
- What roles do fathers play on Neighborhood Street?
- Some areas of Neighborhood Street are scary. How does the author make them seem less scary?
- In what ways is Neighborhood Street like the street you live on? How is it different?
- What evidence is there that suggests the children on Neighborhood Street come from loving families?
- What is left unsaid in the poem titled "House with the Wooden Windows"?

Beyond the Book

- What activities do you have in your community that make your neighborhood special?
- What experiences do you have that deal with a brother (or sister) who always picks a fight?
- What are the required activities and behaviors for a fun overnight?
- Make a list of the stores (businesses), schools, and other public buildings, parks, or playgrounds that make up your neighborhood.
- How many places can you go in your neighborhood without an adult or older sister or brother to go with you?

Books for Further Discussions

The Ant Bully by John Nickle. Scholastic, 1999.

Freedom Summer by Deborah Wiles, illus. by Jerome Lagarrigue. Atheneum, 2001. (CSK–John Steptoe Winner)

The Invisible Princess by Faith Ringgold. Crown, 1999.

The Patchwork Quilt

By Valerie Flournoy,
illus. by Jerry Pinkney
N.Y., Dial, 1985
Grade: K–3
Genre: Fiction
Core Democratic Value:
Common good
Help others at home and school.

Content Perspective

In this story, the making of a patchwork quilt records one year in the life of a family. Tanya grows restless in the house as she recovers from a cold and has to watch as her brothers play outside. Grandma lives with the family and is working on a quilt with scraps of fabric strewn about. As Tanya's interest in the quilt increases, so does her relationship with her grandmother, and as the project grows, so does family involvement until, finally, every member has a place on the quilt. Every member has a secure place in Grandma's heart as well.

Discussion Openers

Students should provide examples of text and/or illustrations to support their responses.

- Why did Tanya decide to help Grandma?
- What effect did Tanya's help have on Grandma?
- What effect did Tanya's decision to help with the quilt have on the rest of the family?
- Why was the quilt so important to Grandma?
- How did Grandma's quilt contribute to the common good?

Beyond the Book

- Choose an illustration from the Coretta Scott King Book Awards Illustrations Gallery, www.ala.org/emiert/coretta-scott-king-book-awards

-illustrations-gallery, that best depicts the core democratic value of the common good. Discuss your reasons for choosing it.

• It is believed that quilts with secret messages may have helped enslaved people escape using the Underground Railroad. Create a secret quilt pattern without words, giving directions from one place to another. Provide classmates with a key to the code and ask them to decipher it.

• Ask elderly family members or friends to tell you what stories from their lives they would want included in a family quilt. What symbols would you use to tell their stories?

• Create a quilt pattern to represent your life. What events would you include?

• Think of a project that your family could do together. With the help of an adult, create a plan to make the project work.

Books for Further Discussions

Nana Upstairs & Nana Downstairs by Tomie dePaola. Putnam, 1973.

Neeny Coming, Neeny Going by Karen English, illus. by Synthia Saint James. BridgeWater, 1996. (CSK Honor)

Storm in the Night by Mary Stolz, illus. by Pat Cummings. Harper & Row, 1988. (CSK Honor)

Uncle Jed's Barbershop by Margaree King Mitchell, illus. by James Ransome. Simon & Schuster, 1993. (CSK Honor)

The Piano Man

By Debbi Chocolate,
illus. by Eric Velasquez
N.Y., Walker, 1998
Grade: K–3
Genre: Fiction/Picture Book
Core Democratic Value: Diversity
Work and play with everyone.

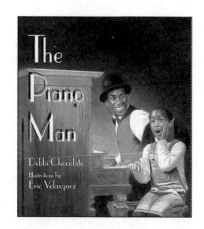

Content Perspective

A young girl recounts the story of her musician grandfather whose skill and mastery of the piano allowed him to play in silent movies, vaudeville, ragtime, and theater. Passing his love of music to daughter and granddaughter, *The Piano Man* leaves a rich musical legacy. The spirited facial expressions depicted in the illustrations give a hint to the grand times his music brought to the listeners.

Discussion Openers

Students should provide examples of text and/or illustrations to support their responses.

- The grandfather in the story played piano for movies without sound. Talk about what it might have been like to see movies without sound.
- Look at the illustration of Dr. Wizard. Tell the story of what is happening in the picture.
- Look at the Piano Man's hands. Look at your hands. How are they the same? How are they different?
- Why did the Piano Man wear an armband? What purpose did it serve?
- Select three pictures and describe the feelings shown in each (e.g., happy, sad, excited, active).

Beyond the Book

- What do you think it was like to have a grandfather who played piano in the old days?
- Talk about the ways the Piano Man changed over the years as music opportunities changed.
- Is this a book that tells a story or a book that gives information? How do you know?
- Look online for information about Scott Joplin and listen to his music. How does it make you feel?
- Watch your favorite movie with the sound off. How did it affect your enjoyment of the story?

Books for Further Discussions

Dizzy by Jonah Winter, illus. by Sean Qualls. Arthur A. Levine, 2006.

Ellington Was Not a Street by Ntozake Shange, illus. by Kadir Nelson. Simon & Schuster, 2004. (CSK Winner)

Jazz by Walter Dean Myers, illus. by Christopher Myers. Holiday House, 2006. (CSK Honor)

Jazz on a Saturday Night by Leo and Diane Dillon. Blue Sky, 2007. (CSK Honor)

My Family Plays Music by Judy Cox, illus. by Elbrite Brown. Holiday House, 2003. (CSK–John Steptoe Winner)

Running the Road to ABC

By Denize Lauture,
illus. by Reynold Ruffins
N.Y., Simon & Schuster, 1996
Grade: K–3
Genre: Picture Book
Core Democratic Value:
Pursuit of Happiness
*Have fun, but follow the rules
at home and school.*

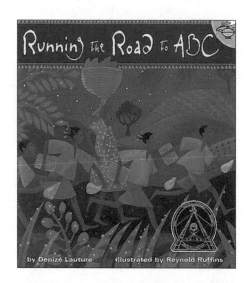

Content Perspective

Running the Road to ABC is a poetic Haitian tale of children eager to get to school on time: running through woods, past the fields, on the road, and through the village. The rhythm of their bare footsteps keep pace with the rhythm of the turtledoves flapping their wings. Boys and girls arrive at school on time and ready to learn their ABCs.

Discussion Openers

Students should provide examples of text and/or illustrations to support their responses.

- What time of day do the children in the story begin their journey to school? How do you know?
- How does their school building in the story compare to the school you attend?
- What evidence is there that reveals how the children in the story feel about going to school?
- Why do you believe the children are in a hurry to get to school?
- Describe the two pictures that show the children running through the town. Look for details about the people, places, or things mentioned or not mentioned in the story.

Beyond the Book

- Think about running or playing outside in your bare feet. What is good or fun about playing barefoot outside? What is not so good?
- Is it important to learn how to read? Why?
- In what ways do you use reading outside of your classroom?
- Do you walk or take the bus to school? Do you run any part of the way? Why or why not?
- What do you carry to school? Describe the items you carry each day that hold your schoolwork and lunch.

Books for Further Discussions

Freedom Summer by Deborah Wiles, illus. by Jerome Lagarrigue. Atheneum, (CSK–John Steptoe Winner)

I Lost My Tooth in Africa by Penda Diakité, illus. by Baba Wagué Diakité. Scholastic, 2006.

Jazz on a Saturday Night by Leo and Diane Dillon. Blue Sky, 2007. (CSK Honor)

My Brother Martin: A Sister Remembers Growing Up with the Rev. Dr. Martin Luther King, Jr. by Christine King Farris, illus. by Chris Soentpiet. Simon & Schuster, 2003.

Virgie Goes to School with Us Boys by Elizabeth Fitzgerald Howard, illus. by E. B. Lewis. Simon & Schuster, 2000. (CSK Honor)

Storm in the Night

By Mary Stolz,
illus. by Pat Cummings
N.Y., Harper & Row, 1988
Grade: K–3
Genre: Contemporary Realistic
Fiction/Picture Book
Core Democratic Value:
Common Good

Work together for the good of all. Accept responsibility for your actions.

Content Perspective

It is a dark and stormy night with "thunder like mountains blowing up." The power is out, it is too dark to read, and of course there will be no TV this night. Mary Stolz creates a perfect scenario for storytelling. Thomas has heard many of his grandfather's stories, some from when he was just a little boy, but this night he hears one his grandfather has not told before. Grandfather relates a story, a true story, about one stormy night when his dog disappeared and he was too frightened to go looking for him. The dialogue between Thomas and his grandfather is wonderfully realistic. Pat Cummings's illustrations, filtered through a dark blue lens, create a calming contrast to the storm raging just beyond their porch steps.

Discussion Openers

Students should provide examples of text and/or illustrations to support their responses.

- Why did Grandfather decide to tell this particular story?
- Why was Grandfather's dog left outside?
- What did Grandfather learn about responsibility from his childhood experience?
- How can you tell that Thomas trusted Grandfather?

- What do Pat Cummings's illustrations tell you about Thomas and Grandfather that is not included in the text?

Beyond the Book

- What choice would you have made if your pet had been left out in a storm?
- With your eyes open, sit quietly and make a list of all the sounds around you.
- Turn off all the lights in your house, turn off all computers, and make sure the TV is off. Close your eyes and sit quietly. Listen for sounds. After several minutes, open your eyes and write down what you heard. How are the sounds different from what you heard when all the power was on and your eyes were open?
- Research storms online and list five things that you didn't know about lightning and thunder.
- Create your own story about a dark and stormy night.

Books for Further Discussions

The Chicken-Chasing Queen of Lamar County by Janice N. Harrington, illus. by Shelley Jackson. Farrar, Straus and Giroux, 2007.

Growing Up with Tamales = Los Tamales de Ana by Gwendolyn Zepeda, illus. by April Ward, Spanish translation by Gabriela Baeza Ventura. Houston, Tex. : Piñata Books, 2008.

Justin and the Best Biscuits in the World by Mildred Pitts Walter, illus. by Catherine Stock. Lothrop, Lee and Shepard, 1986. (CSK Winner)

Ogbo: Sharing Life in an African Village by Ifeoma Onyefulu. Gulliver Books, 1996.

Uncle Jed's Barbershop by Margaree King Mitchell, illus. by James Ransome. Scholastic, 1993. (CSK Honor)

Tar Beach

By Faith Ringgold
N.Y., Crown/Random House, 1991
Grade: K–3
Genre: Historical Fiction/Picture Book
Core Democratic Value: Equality
Give everyone an equal chance.

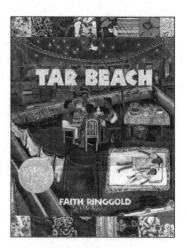

Content Perspective

It is 1939 when eight-year-old Cassie Louise Lightfoot discovers she can fly: "All you need is somewhere to go that you can't get to any other way." In so doing, she acknowledges all the things that seem just out of reach: the diamond necklace that was the bridge her father helped build and that opened on the day she was born, ice cream every day, a union job for her father who helped build the Union Building yet was excluded from union membership because of his color and heritage. As Cassie and her brother, Be Be, fly above the city, Cassie claims all of those things and exclaims with youthful confidence, "I am free to go wherever I want for the rest of my life." Faith Ringgold's exuberant illustrations explode across the double-page spreads inviting all of us to fly with Cassie into a new world where freedom and equality are a given.

Discussion Openers

Students should provide examples of text and/or illustrations to support their responses.

- Why was the George Washington Bridge so important to Cassie?
- Flying suggests a type of freedom. What freedoms did Cassie claim while she flew?
- Using Faith Ringgold's illustrations, create a story about Cassie's family.
- How is Cassie's family like your own family? How is it different?
- Why did Faith Ringgold call this story *Tar Beach*?

- If you could meet Faith Ringgold, what question would you ask her about *Tar Beach?*

Beyond the Book

- Listen to Martin Luther King, Jr.'s "I Have a Dream" speech. How is his dream similar to Cassie's?
- List words in the story that are not familiar to you. How can you determine the meaning from the story?
- If you could fly, where would you go?
- Have you ever wanted to be part of a team but were rejected by other team members? How did it make you feel?
- Did you ever deliberately exclude someone from your team? How did that make you feel?

Books for Further Discussions

Aunt Harriet's Underground Railroad in the Sky by Faith Ringgold. Crown, 1992. (Jane Addams Winner)

The Great Migration: Journey to the North by Eloise Greenfield, illus. by Jan Spivey Gilchrist. HarperCollins/Amistad, 2011. (CSK Honor)

The Invisible Princess by Faith Ringgold. Crown, 1999.

The People Could Fly: The Picture Book by Virginia Hamilton, illus. by Leo and Diane Dillon. Knopf, 2004. (CSK Honor)

Underground: Finding the Light to Freedom by Shane W. Evans. Roaring Brook, 2011. (CSK Winner)

Uncle Jed's Barbershop

By Margaree King Mitchell,
illus. by James Ransome
N.Y., Simon & Schuster, 1993
Grade: K–3
Genre: Picture Book
Core Democratic Value: Common Good
Help others.

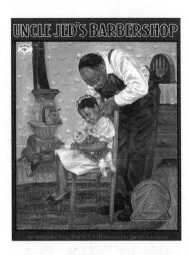

Content Perspective

The realities of life in the segregated South do not prevent Uncle Jed from dreaming of owning his own barbershop. Neither the difficulties of saving money when earnings were so meager nor the necessity of providing the funds for the emergency surgery needed by his favorite niece stop him from dreaming. Uncle Jed saved and saved, sometimes only pennies, before he was finally able to realize the dream of owning his own barbershop.

Discussion Openers

Students should provide examples of text and/or illustrations to support their responses.

- Look at the first picture in the book. Describe the scene. Pay attention to the feelings expressed in the faces of the characters.
- List five new words you learned from the book. Write the dictionary meanings of the words.
- Choose one illustration from the middle of the book and one from the end. Describe what is going on.
- What season is it in the story? How do you know?
- Share with your classmates three ways that made Uncle Jed's dream all the more deserving.

Beyond the Book

- Farmers in the story often wore overalls. Describe three different uniforms worn by workers today.
- What is meant by *street clothes*?
- Explain the terms *segregation* and *integration*.
- Do you have a dream about your future life? Share your dream with your classmates.
- Have you ever been to a barbershop or beauty shop? Draw a picture of the items typically found in barbershops or beauty shops.

Books for Further Discussions

Freedom Summer by Deborah Wiles, illus. by Jerome Lagarrigue. Atheneum, 2001. (CSK–John Steptoe).

Harvesting Hope: The Story of Cesar Chavez by Kathleen Krull, illus. by Yuyi Morales. Harcourt, 2003. (Pura Belpre Winner, Woodson Winner, Jane Addams Winner)

Hot, Hot Roti for Dada-ji by F. Zia, illus. by Ken Min. Lee & Low, 2011.

The Invisible Princess by Faith Ringgold. Crown, 1999.

My Brother Martin: A Sister Remembers Growing Up with the Rev. Dr. Martin Luther King, Jr. by Christine King Farris, illus. by Chris Soentpiet. Simon & Schuster, 2003.

Underground: Finding the Light to Freedom

By Shane W. Evans
N.Y., Roaring Brook, 2011
Grade: K–3
Genre: Nonfiction
Core Democratic Value:
Liberty/Personal Freedom
Follow your beliefs and let others follow theirs.

Content Perspective

Families with children are running for their lives. Armed men chase them on horseback with bright lanterns. Previously enslaved, they now dream of a better life, so they run. They crawl. They are afraid but very brave. The Underground Railroad is a path to freedom and safety. Some make it; some don't. With few words and telling pictures, Shane W. Evans brings to life the treacherous road to freedom. Filled with a sliver of moonlight and bright stars, his illustrations extend the sparse words that tell this important story so even very young children will understand.

Discussion Openers

Students should provide examples of text and/or illustrations to support their responses.

- Stars and the moon play an important role in *Underground*. Look at the illustrations and decide how they might be harmful and how they might be helpful.
- Using the Shane W. Evans's illustrations, select three pictures and write new details about the story.
- Identify the illustration that portrays when the runaways were in the most danger. Tell their story.
- What is meant by the statement, "Some don't make it?"

- Write a poem about freedom based on the story by Shane W. Evans. Illustrate it with your own pictures.
- What threats did the environment present to the runaways?

Beyond the Book

- Have you ever had an experience that was really scary? Write and illustrate your story.
- People using the Underground Railroad depended on other people to help them get to freedom. Whom can you depend on if you need help?
- What can you do to help someone who is afraid?
- The behavior of people chasing escaped slaves was very scary. Did your behavior ever scare someone? How did it make you feel?
- Shane W. Evans uses the moon and stars to illuminate his story. The North Star and the Big Dipper were useful to those escaping slavery. Try to locate them on a starry night.

Books for Further Discussions

Dave the Potter: Artist, Poet, Slave by Laban Carrick Hill, illus. by Bryan Collier. Little, Brown, 2010. (CSK Winner, Caldecott Honor, Woodson Honor)

Freedom Summer by Deborah Wiles, illus. by Jerome Lagarrigue. Atheneum, 2001. (CSK–John Steptoe Winner)

Harvesting Hope: The Story of Cesar Chavez by Kathleen Krull, illus. by Yuyi Morales. Harcourt, 2003. (Pura Belpre Honor, Woodson Honor, Jane Addams Winner)

Moses: When Harriet Tubman Led Her People to Freedom by Carole Boston Weatherford, illus. by Kadir Nelson. Hyperion/Jump at the Sun, 2006. (CSK Winner, Caldecott Honor)

When Harriet Met Sojourner by Catherine Clinton, illus. by Shane W. Evans. HarperCollins/Amistad, 2007.

Uptown

By Bryan Collier
N.Y., Henry Holt, 2000
Grade: K–3
Genre: Fiction/Picture Book
Core Democratic Value: Common Good
Help others. People should work together
for the good of all.

Content Perspective

The pride and love of a community is portrayed with cut paper-and-collage illustrations. Bryan Collier shares the many aspects of his hometown. The reader is transported into Collier's world of food, art, music, community, fabrics, and brownstone houses. Reds, yellows, greens, and blues provide a visual feast that invites the reader in.

Discussion Openers

Students should provide examples of text and/or illustrations to support their responses.

- Some say the brownstone houses look to be made of chocolate. Do you agree? Why or why not?
- What other pictures might Mr. Collier have included that show the work grown-ups do in a city?
- Look at the pictures of the girls going to church. They are walking. Are there places that you and your friends walk rather than ride? Why or why not?
- Look up the Boys Choir of Harlem. Share three interesting facts about the group with your classmates.
- Select a picture from the book and write your own story about it.

Beyond the Book

- Create a collage of your street using brightly colored paper shapes.
- Draw a map that shows where important buildings in your neighborhood are located.
- *Brownstone* is a term that describes a specific type of housing. *Highrise* and *bungalow* are also specific types of homes. Is there a name for the type of home you live in?
- What do you like best about your neighborhood? Tell and illustrate your neighborhood story.
- Research African fabrics online. Look for examples in your community.

Books for Further Discussions

Freedom Summer by Deborah Wiles, illus. by Jerome Lagarrigue. Atheneum, 2001. (CSK–John Steptoe Winner)

Hot Day on Abbott Avenue by Karen English, illus. by Javaka Steptoe. Clarion, 2004. (Jane Addams Winner)

Stuff!: Reduce, Reuse, Recycle by Steven Kroll, illus. by Steve Cox. Marshall Cavendish, 2009.

The Worst of Friends: Thomas Jefferson, John Adams, and the True Story of an American Feud by Suzanne Tripp Jurmain, illus. by Larry Day. Dutton, 2011.

Virgie Goes to School with Us Boys

By Elizabeth Fitzgerald Howard,
illus. by E. B. Lewis
N.Y., Simon & Schuster, 2000
Grade: K–3
Genre: Historical Fiction/Picture Book
Core Democratic Value: Equality
Give everyone an equal chance.

Content Perspective

"Virgie was always begging to go to school with us boys. All summer long she kept asking and asking." She was ready to tackle the seven-mile trek, even if she had to go through a dark and dangerous forest. The Civil War is over, and this formerly enslaved family is free to carve their own lives from the ruins. Virgie's parents know that education is key to prosperity for boys. Virgie convinces them that girls need education, too. The poignant illustrations of E. B. Lewis extend the story with portrayals of the hardworking farm family and of the character and determination of the children.

Discussion Openers

Students should provide examples of text and/or illustrations to support their responses.

- What character traits did CC exhibit that made him a responsible member of the family?
- What reasons did Nelson give that Virgie should not go to school with the boys?
- Nelson changed his mind about Virgie by the time they arrived at school. What made him think differently about her?
- Why was education of primary importance to Virgie's family? What did an education enable newly freed people to do?
- What purpose do the monsters, Raw Head and Bloody Bones, serve in the story?

Beyond the Book

- Explore the origins of the monsters, Raw Head and Bloody Bones.
- The artist Vermeer painted a picture called "The Milkmaid." Compare Vermeer's painting with E. B. Lewis's illustration of the children's mother preparing food and clothing for the long trek to school.
- After the Civil War, new black citizens were filled with hope for the future. Choose a noted black historical figure who demonstrates the realization of that hope.
- What would your life be like if you were not allowed to go to school?
- Ask an adult why he or she thinks education is important. Share what you find out with your classmates.

Books for Further Discussions

Dave the Potter: Artist, Poet, Slave by Laban Carrick Hill, illus. by Bryan Collier. Little, Brown, 2010. (CSK Winner, Woodson Honor, Caldecott Honor)

Freedom River by Doreen Rappaport, illus. by Bryan Collier. Hyperion/Jump at the Sun, 2000. (CSK Honor)

Freedom Summer by Deborah Wiles, illus. by Jerome Lagarrigue. Atheneum, 2001. (CSK–John Steptoe Winner)

Moses: When Harriet Tubman Led Her People to Freedom by Carole Boston Weatherford, illus. by Kadir Nelson. Hyperion/Jump at the Sun, 2006. (CSK Winner, Caldecott Honor)

Rosa by Nikki Giovanni, illus. by Bryan Collier. Henry Holt, 2005. (Caldecott Honor, CSK Winner)

Working Cotton

By Sherley Anne Williams,
illus. by Carole Byard
N.Y., Harcourt, 1992
Grade: K–3
Genre: Contemporary Realistic
Fiction/Picture Book
Core Democratic Value: Common good
Help others at home and school.

Content Perspective

Shelan's parents are migrant workers in the cotton fields of central California. As narrator in *Working Cotton,* she gives an account of daily life that begins before sunrise and ends after dark. It is an effort that involves the entire family, and it is grueling work. Yet the family stays together in the fields, where "Mama sing; Daddy hum." They are ever hopeful that the weather will continue to cooperate and bring them luck. Carole Byard's rich illustrations fill the pages with the reality of working cotton: children in the fields, mothers and fathers dripping with sweat, working together, getting through the day.

Discussion Openers

Students should provide examples of text and/or illustrations to support their responses.

- Make a list of everything that you do for one day. Compare it to Shelan's day. What differences are there?
- What do you dream about? What are Shelan's dreams?
- Look at the illustrations. How do Shelan's mother and father show that they care about their children?
- Why do you think a family would choose this life?
- Think of ways that this story relates to the core democratic value of the common good?

Beyond the Book

- What contributions do farmworkers make to the United States?
- What would happen if there were no farmworkers?
- What is the Harvest of Hope Foundation (www.harvestofhope.net /about-harvest-of-hope.php)?
- List three things that you would like to know about farms in your area. Visit a local farm market with an adult family member and ask a worker your questions. Write a paragraph about what you find out.
- Make a list of your favorite farm-grown foods. What health benefits do these foods provide?

Books for Further Discussions

Amelia's Road by Linda Jacobs Altman, illus. by Enrique O. Sanchez. Lee & Low, 1993.

Going Home by Eve Bunting, illus. by David Diaz. HarperCollins, 1996.

Harvesting Hope: The Story of Cesar Chavez by Kathleen Krull, illus. by Yuyi Morales. Harcourt, 2003. (Jane Addams Winner, Pura Belpre Honor, Woodson Honor).

Lights on the River by Jane Resh Thomas, illus. by Michael Dooling. Hyperion, 1994.

Tomás and the Library Lady by Pat Mora, illus. by Raúl Colón. Knopf, 1997.

CHAPTER 2

Grades 2–4

The Bells of Christmas

By Virginia Hamilton,
illus. by Lambert Davis
N.Y., Harcourt, 1989
Grade: 2–4
Genre: Historical Fiction
Core Democratic Value: Common Good
People should work together for the good of all.

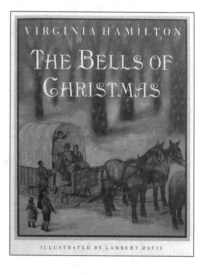

Content Perspective

Virginia Hamilton brings her exceptional storytelling skills to this 1890 Christmas story that takes place along the historic National Road near Springfield, Ohio. Her characterization is rich, as members of this close-knit family spring to life through the period illustrations of Lambert Davis. Warm memories of a childhood when transportation by horse and carriage was still the norm and family responsibility was a given, anchor this story in its historical perspective. She also cleverly provides a subtle example of how mechanization began to infiltrate this nineteenth-century community. The joy of an unexpected snowfall brings to life the hopefulness of the season. The snowfall, the safe arrival of relatives, and the greetings of neighbors combine to create a strong sense of family and community working together for the common good. This extraordinary Christmas story offers many opportunities for discussion.

Discussion Openers

Students should provide examples of text and/or illustrations to support their responses.

- Jason's family had a pattern of working together. How were tasks divided? Describe the benefits of working together. Were there any downsides?
- Give examples of how Jason's family contributed to the larger community.
- Was there anything in this story that surprised you? Explain.
- The story is told from Jason's perspective. How would it be different if Lissy told the story?
- Explain the meaning of the statement, "The meal made our long supper table groan."
- How did Virginia Hamilton introduce mechanical things into her story?
- Why did Jason want his Papa to look just like everyone else?

Beyond the Book

- Research the Industrial Revolution. (www.kidsdiscover.com /industrial-revolution-for-kids) Name two important machines that were invented during this time.
- Make a list of all the mechanical things that you see in one day. How do they help the community? How might they harm the community?
- List the mechanical things in your home. Try going one day without using any of them and write a short essay about what it was like.

- Christmas is celebrated in many different ways. Choose a country other than your own and research how Christmas is celebrated there.
- Ask an elderly family member or friend to tell you about how he or she celebrated holidays as a child. Compare it to how you celebrate them today.

Books for Further Discussions

A Chanukah Noel: A True Story by Sharon Jennings, illus. by Gillian Newland. Second Story, 2010.

Christmas in the Big House, Christmas in the Quarters by Patricia C. McKissack and Fredrick L. McKissack, illus. by John Thompson. Scholastic, 1994. (CSK Winner, Orbis Pictus Honor)

Crossing Bok Chitto: A Choctaw Tale of Friendship & Freedom by Tim Tingle, illus. by Jeanne Rorex Bridges. Cinco Puntos, 2006. (American Indian Youth Literature Winner)

Selavi, That Is Life: A Haitian Story of Hope by Youme. Cinco Puntos, 2004. (Jane Addams Winner)

Bird

By Zetta Elliott,
illus. by Shadra Strickland
N.Y., Lee & Low, 2008
Grade: 2–4
Genre: Contemporary Realistic
Fiction/Poetry
Core Democratic Value: Rule of Law
Rules are made for everyone to follow.

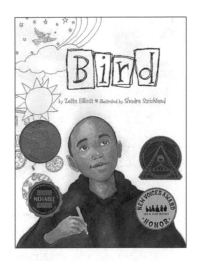

Content Perspective

Mehkai is a young boy living in a middle-class urban setting. Granddad nicknamed him Bird because when he was just a baby he would open his mouth just like a baby bird chirping for food. Bird is fascinated by birds and goes to the park with his Granddad's friend, Uncle Son, to feed them and draw pictures of them. His parents work and his older brother, Marcus, can no longer accept the responsibility of looking after Bird when he returns from school. Marcus is a drug addict. One Sunday when Bird's family returns from church, they discover that all of their belongings have been removed from the house, including all of Mama's jewelry. The next day, the locks are changed and Marcus is no longer allowed in the house. When Marcus shows up, Bird is faced with the dilemma of whether or not to open the door to him. Through his friendship with Uncle Son, Bird eventually learns that "some broken things can't be fixed."

Discussion Openers

Students should provide examples of text and/or illustrations to support their responses.

- What clues can you point to that tell the reader about the community where Bird's family lives?
- Who is Uncle Son and why is he in the story?
- What do the illustrations tell us about Marcus?

- Bird loves his big brother dearly. Do you believe he will follow his brother's lead? Why or why not?
- How do the illustrations help the reader to understand the kind of person Marcus was?
- Bird's brother, Marcus, lost his battle with drug addiction despite the support of his family. What are the good memories his family might wish to hold on to?

Beyond the Book

- Brooklyn is the setting for Bird's life. Think about what your neighborhood is like and draw a picture that shows the places that are important to you.
- Bird's brother, Marcus, shared his love of art with Bird. What have you learned from close relatives? Write a thank-you note to someone who has taught you something.
- Birds are used as a metaphor. What is a metaphor? Can you find other metaphors in the text and art?
- Research an African American illustrator. Discuss what motivated him or her to illustrate books for children.
- Is there anyone in your life who does not live with you but provides you with guidance? In what way do they support you?

Books for Further Discussions

Freedom River by Doreen Rappaport, illus. by Bryan Collier. Hyperion/ Jump at the Sun, 2000. (CSK Honor)

Freedom Summer by Deborah Wiles. Atheneum, 2001. (CSK–John Steptoe Winner)

Goin' Someplace Special by Patricia C. McKissack. Atheneum, 2001. (CSK Winner)

Wind Flyers by Angela Johnson, illus. by Loren Long. Simon & Schuster, 2007.

The Great Migration: Journey to the North

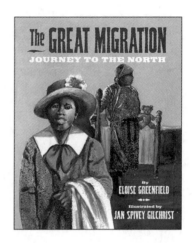

By Eloise Greenfield,
illus. by Jan Spivey Gilchrist
N.Y., HarperCollins/Amistad, 2011

Grade: 2–4

Genre: Nonfiction

Core Democratic Value: Equality

Give everyone an equal chance.

Content Perspective

Eloise Greenfield was just four months old when her family moved from Parmele, North Carolina, to Washington, D.C., a great journey north and away from oppressive Jim Crow laws. They were one family among more than a million African Americans leaving their homes and the terror of the Ku Klux Klan behind. Eloise Greenfield captures the intense feelings of family members with lively language, a perfect introduction to the Great Migration for young readers. Jan Spivey Gilchrist's illustrations vividly support each poem with images that seem to emerge from history with ethereal wonder and immediacy. People are on the move not out of desperation, but more from determination to find a better place.

Discussion Openers

Students should provide examples of text and/or illustrations to support their responses.

- Read the first poem, "The News." What caused the family to talk about moving? What does the illustration tell you about this particular family?
- Read the second poem. Why was it so hard for this man to say goodbye? How does the illustration help you understand his feelings?
- Identify the poem and illustration that best depicts the reasons for leaving the South. Explain why you chose that particular poem.
- What ideas justified the Great Migration?
- In your own words tell the story of Girl and Boy.

Beyond the Book

- Explore the Great Migration online at: www.digitalhistory.uh.edu /database/article_display.cfm?HHID=443.
- What effect did the Great Migration have on the cities in the North?
- What effect did the Great Migration have on the South?
- African Americans did not find the freedoms that they hoped for in the North. Why not?
- What housing laws were put in place to exclude African Americans?
- Have you ever been excluded from an activity or not chosen to play on a particular team? Explain how it felt.
- Have you ever excluded a classmate from joining an activity or team? How did it make you feel?

Books for Further Discussions

Going North by Janice N. Harrington, illus. by Jerome Lagarrigue. Melanie Kroupa, 2004.

The Great Migration: An American Story. Paintings by Jacob Lawrence with a poem by Walter Dean Myers. HarperCollins, 1993. (Woodson Honor)

Moses: When Harriet Tubman Led Her People to Freedom by Carole Boston Weatherford, illus. by Kadir Nelson. Hyperion/Jump at the Sun, 2006. (CSK Winner, Caldecott Honor)

When Harriet Met Sojourner by Catherine Clinton, illus. by Shane W. Evans. HarperCollins/Amistad, 2007.

Jimi Sounds Like a Rainbow: A Story of the Young Jimi Hendrix

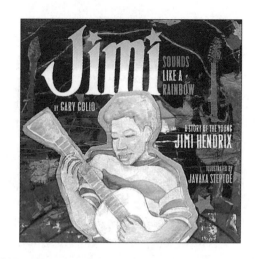

By Gary Golio,
illus. by Javaka Steptoe
Boston, Clarion, 2010
Grade: 2–4
Genre: Picture Book Biography
Core Democratic Value: Pursuit of Happiness
All people can find happiness in their own way, as long as they do not step on the rights of others.

Content Perspective

Layered mixed-media illustrations by Javaka Steptoe provide insights into the evolving musical genius of Jimi Hendrix from his early youth to adulthood. As colorful and unique as Hendrix himself, the pictures bring to life the story of a young man who integrates all that he sees around him into his remarkable interpretations of social and environmental influences on his music.

Discussion Openers

Students should provide examples of text and/or illustrations to support their responses.

- Jimi was different from most of his neighbors and classmates. What evidence can you find to support this?
- What evidence in the illustrations shows Jimi's awareness of the smallest details in his surroundings?
- What does Jimi's willingness to practice and practice tell you about him as a person? What is the message in Jimi's words: "Don't let nobody turn you off from your own thoughts and dreams"?
- In what ways do the illustrations reflect the title?

Beyond the Book

- Research the history of the guitar. What kinds of music do you think of most often when you think of the guitar?
- Research Jimi Hendrix, his life and his music.
- Research Javaka Steptoe's career as an artist and illustrator. What similarities do you find between Javaka and Jimi?
- Find evidence from your reading to support the idea that willingness to practice, commitment to do the work, strength to face obstacles, and refusal to give up are key to success.
- What is a genius, musical or otherwise?

Books for Further Discussions

Before John Was a Jazz Giant by Carole Boston Weatherford, illus. by Sean Qualls. Henry Holt, 2008. (CSK Honor)

Duke Ellington: The Piano Prince and His Orchestra by Andrea Davis Pinkney, illus. by Brian Pinkney. Hyperion/Jump at the Sun, 1998. (CSK Honor, Caldecott Honor)

Ellington Was Not a Street by Ntozake Shange, illus. by Kadir Nelson. Simon & Schuster, 2004. (CSK Winner)

My Family Plays Music by Judy Cox, illus. by Elbrite Brown. Holiday House, 2003. (CSK–John Steptoe Winner)

The Secret Olivia Told Me

By N. Joy, illus. by Nancy Devard
East Orange, N.J., Just Us Books,
2007
Grade: 2–4
Genre: Fiction/Picture Book
Core Democratic Value: Justice
Take turns and be fair to others.
Included are the values of honesty and trustworthiness.

Content Perspective

Olivia's secret is so big that even a promise cannot contain it. As her secret accidently slips out, it spreads and grows with each retelling. A friendship is about to disintegrate; will an apology be enough to save it? The black silhouettes heighten the drama of this story while the ever-expanding red balloon emphasizes the importance of trust and the possible consequences of breaking that trust.

Discussion Openers

Students should provide examples of text and/or illustrations to support their responses.

- Why did Olivia's friend reveal the secret that she was told?
- Why did Olivia feel she could trust her friend to keep her secret?
- How did Olivia's friend feel after she revealed the secret?
- How did Olivia feel when she found out that her friend had revealed her secret?
- When is it okay to reveal a secret?

Beyond the Book

- Play the game Whisper a Secret.
  - » Children sit in a line.
  - » The first person whispers a message to the person next to them.
  - » That person whispers the message to the next person.
  - » Continue until the last person has heard the message.
  - » Compare the first message to the last message.
  - » Has the original message changed? How?

- Examine the illustrations and layout of the book from beginning to end. Do the jacket and cover invite you to open the book? How does the typeface change to emphasize certain words? How do text and illustration work together to add excitement and mystery to the telling of the story?
- The main point of interest, where the eye is drawn, is called the focal point. Where is the eye drawn most often in Devard's illustrations?

Books for Further Discussions

Freedom Summer by Deborah Wiles, illus. by Jerome Lagarrigue. Atheneum, 2001. (CSK–John Steptoe Winner)

Harvesting Hope: The Story of Cesar Chavez by Kathleen Krull, illus. by Yuyi Morales. Harcourt, 2003. (Pura Belpre Honor, Woodson Honor, Jane Addams Winner)

Martin's Big Words: The Life of Dr. Martin Luther King, Jr. by Doreen Rappaport, illus. by Bryan Collier. Hyperion/Jump at the Sun, 2002. (CSK Honor, Caldecott Honor, Jane Addams Winner, Orbis Pictus Honor)

Meet Danitra Brown by Nikki Grimes, illus. by Floyd Cooper. Lothrop, Lee and Shepard, 1994. (CSK Honor)

Nasreen's Secret School: A True Story from Afghanistan by Jeanette Winter. Beach Lane, 2009. (Jane Addams Winner)

The Secret Keeper by Kate Coombs, illus. by Heather M. Solomon. Atheneum, 2006.

Seeds of Change

By Jen Cullerton Johnson,
illus. by Sonia Lynn Sadler
N.Y., Lee & Low, 2010
Grade: 2–4
Genre: Biography
Core Democratic Value: Common Good
People should work for the good of all.

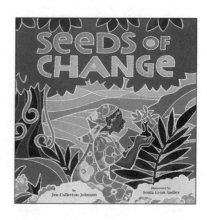

Content Perspective

This inspiring biography of female environmentalist Wangari Maathai depicts the founding of the Greenbelt Movement in 1977, for which she received the Nobel Peace Prize. The scratchboard-and-oil illustrations feature dominant white outlines that make a strikingly stylized book. The abundance of green complements the theme of the story. Scientist and activist, Wangari, also known as Mama Miti, held on to her belief in equal rights for women and respect for the land.

Discussion Openers

Students should provide examples of text and/or illustrations to support their responses.

- What do you think Wangari Maathai meant by the statement, "Young people, you are our hope and our future"?
- Why is it significant that Wangari received her first environmental lesson from her mother?
- Where many might have given up upon seeing the government sell off the rights to Kenya's land, Wangari did not. What kept her going?
- How are the title of the book and Wangari's determination to plant trees related?
- What does Wangari's decision to return to the country of her birth say about her as a scholar and leader?

Beyond the Book

- Identify three outstanding African American or female scientists, activists, or world leaders. Select three things that impressed you about their lives.
- Locate Kenya on a map. What countries surround it and what other information does the map provide about this area of the world?
- Think about why women's rights were so intertwined with the work Wangari did in both Kenya and the United States. Compare her work in Kenya with her work in the United States.
- Think about the practice of governments in countries like Kenya selling off the rights to natural resources to foreign buyers. What might be good about it? Why might it not be so good?
- Make a list of ways you and your classmates can show respect for our environment.

Books for Further Discussions

An Apple for Harriet Tubman by Glennette Tilley Turner, illus. by Susan Keeter. Albert Whitman, 2006.

Let It Shine: Stories of Black Women Freedom Fighters by Andrea Davis Pinkney, illus. by Stephen Alcorn. Harcourt, 2000. (CSK, Woodson)

Sojourner Truth's Step-Stomp Stride by Andrea Davis Pinkney, illus. by Brian Pinkney. Hyperion/Jump at the Sun, 2009. (Jane Addams)

When Harriet Met Sojourner by Catherine Clinton, illus. by Shane W. Evans. HarperCollins/Amistad, 2007.

Thunder Rose

By Jerdine Nolen, illus. by Kadir Nelson
N.Y., Harcourt, 2003

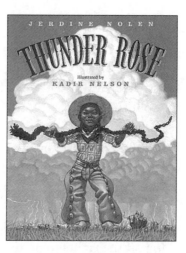

Grade: 2–4
Genre: Folktale
Core Democratic Value: Common Good
Help others.

Content Perspective

Kadir Nelson's oil-and-watercolor paintings depict the exploits of larger-than-life
Thunder Rose. Author Jerdine Nolen created this smart, sassy, stronger-
than-a-bull heroine. She tells a tale of the West in the tradition of John
Henry and Paul Bunyan—a tale that gives hope and encouragement to
those struggling to find their place in the world.

Discussion Openers

Students should provide examples of text and/or illustrations to support
their responses.

- Select your favorite picture of Thunder Rose as a child. Share with
  classmates why you chose this picture.
- In what ways did Thunder Rose help others?
- Give Thunder Rose a different name that reflects ways that she
  worked for the common good. Support your choice by listing three
  reasons why you chose the name.
- Look at the first picture in the story. Why did Kadir Nelson select that
  particular image as the first illustration?
- Make a list of words and phrases that describe Thunder Rose's
  extraordinary exploits.

Beyond the Book

- Use online resources to research blacks in the American West. Look for heroines like Shotgun Mary, born a slave in Tennessee in 1832.
- Author Jerdine Nolen did not tell the reader much about what foods Rose ate. Create a week's menu of breakfasts for Thunder Rose.
- Make a list of the places named in the story. Use online resources to provide three facts about one of the places on your list.
- In what ways is Thunder Rose's life different from yours?
- Pick a word that describes you and add it to your name (e.g., Dancing Dan or Rachel the Reader).

Books for Further Discussions

Doña Flor: A Tall Tale About a Giant Woman with a Great Big Heart by Pat Mora, illus. by Raúl Colón. Knopf, 2005. (Pura Belpre Winner/ Honor)

John Henry by Julius Lester, illus. by Brian Pinkney. Dial, 1994. (Caldecott Honor)

Justin and the Best Biscuits in the World by Mildred Pitts Walter, illus. by Catherine Stock. Lothrop, Lee and Shepard, 1986.

My Rows and Piles of Coins by Tololwa M. Mollel, illus. by E. B. Lewis. Clarion, 1999. (CSK Honor)

CHAPTER 3

Grades 3–6

Almost to Freedom

By Vaunda Micheaux Nelson,
illus. by Colin Bootman
N.Y., Carolrhoda, 2003

Grade: 3–5
Genre: Historical Fiction/Picture Book
Core Democratic Value: Liberty
*Liberty includes the freedom to believe
what you want, to choose your own
friends, to have your own ideas and
opinions, to express your ideas in public, to meet in groups, and to have any
lawful job or business.*

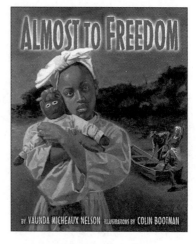

Content Perspective

The cruel realities of life as a slave are told through the voice of Sally,
the doll created from scrap cloth by Miz Rachel for her daughter, Lindy.

Sally and Lindy are inseparable until something important happens. Miz Rachel awakens Lindy in the middle of the night with the words: "Hurry now, but hush." Before Lindy realizes what is happening, she and her mother are running—no, they are flying through the night. The belief that they could achieve a life not dictated by others sustained their purposeful journey. Illustrator Colin Bootman captures the tension of the escape with dazzling color. Accents of yellow throughout offer glimpses of hope that Sally and Lindy will be reunited.

Discussion Openers

Students should provide examples of text and/or illustrations to support their responses.

- Choose three pictures and describe how the characters might have felt.
- Make a KWL (what I know, what I want to know, and what I learned) chart for the story.
- What freedoms did Lindy and her family have on the plantation where they were enslaved?
- Why was the doll, Sally, so important to Lindy?
- Describe what is happening in the last picture of the story.
- What role did the woman in the silver hair play in the story?
- Why did Lindy's desire to spell her name result in a beating by the overseer?

Beyond the Book

- Write a different ending for the story.
- Search online resources for the history of African American ragdolls. Create a ragdoll for hospitalized children.
- If you were forced to leave your home, what one thing would you take with you? Support your choice.
- Research life on a southern plantation during the 1800s. Identify three specific constraints to an enslaved person's freedom to choose.
- How were enslaved people able to plan for escape in spite of the constraints of plantation life?

Books for Further Discussions

Freedom River by Doreen Rappaport, illus. by Bryan Collier. Hyperion/
Jump at the Sun, 2000. (CSK Honor)

Minty: A Story of Young Harriet Tubman by Alan Schroeder, illus. by
Jerry Pinkney. Dial, 1996. (CSK Winner)

Only Passing Through: The Story of Sojourner Truth by Anne Rockwell,
illus. by R. Gregory Christie. Knopf, 2000. (CSK Honor, Orbis Pictus Recommended)

Bad News for Outlaws: The Remarkable Life of Bass Reeves, Deputy U.S. Marshal

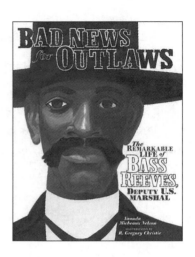

By Vaunda Micheaux Nelson,
illus. by R. Gregory Christie
N.Y., Carolrhoda, 2009

Grade: 3–6

Genre: Biography

Core Democratic Value: Rule of Law

Both the government and the people must obey the law.

Content Perspective

Bass Reeves, fearless lawman of the American West, is bigger than life in this well-researched, rip-roaring biography. Employing colorful terms and short, powerful sentences, this narrative introduces young readers to the fearless, dependable, African American straight shooter who kept the peace in Indian territory for thirty-two years. R. Gregory Christie's rich illustrations capture the intelligence and wit of this extraordinary character's life. *Bad News for Outlaws* will captivate readers of all ages, and the rich endnotes will provide places to learn about outlaws and lawmen alike.

Discussion Openers

Students should provide examples of text and/or illustrations to support their responses.

- What ideas justify Marshal Bass Reeves's killing of Jim Web?
- What qualities did Reeves exhibit that made him a good lawman?
- When Bass Reeves was a slave, his mother thought he might turn out bad. Why?

- The West was a lawless place by the time the Civil War ended. The rule of law was not yet established there. What happens when people live without rules or laws? What does the law provide?
- What ideas justify the U.S. government sending the hanging judge to bring law to this vast territory?
- Why was Bass Reeves both respected and hated?
- What made Bass Reeves a good citizen?

Beyond the Book

- Look up Belle Starr online. Why was she called the Bandit Queen?
- Research the life of Judge Isaac C. Parker (the hanging judge) online. What made him a good choice to bring law and order to the West?
- When writing a biography, the author selects aspects of the subject's life that seem significant. Explore the life of Bass Reeves online. Discover more facts about his life not covered in *Bad News for Outlaws*.
- Make a list of rules in your school that help keep order. What effect do they have on your school day?
- If there were a Bass Reeves Award, who would receive it in your school? Why?
- What is your personal responsibility for keeping order in your school?

Books for Further Discussions

Claudette Colvin: Twice Toward Justice by Phillip Hoose. Farrar/Kroupa, 2009. (Jane Addams Honor, Newbery Honor, Sibert Honor, Woodson Winner)

One Crazy Summer by Rita Williams-Garcia. HarperCollins/Amistad, 2010. (CSK Winner, Newbery Honor)

Rosa by Nikki Giovanni, illus. by Bryan Collier. Henry Holt, 2005. (Caldecott Honor, CSK Winner)

We Troubled the Waters by Ntozake Shange, illus. by Rod Brown. HarperCollins/Amistad, 2009.

Brendan Buckley's Universe and Everything in It

By Sundee T. Frazier
N.Y., Delacorte/Random House, 2007

Grade: 4–6

Genre: Contemporary Realistic Fiction

Core Democratic Value: Diversity

Differences in language, dress, food, national origin, race, and religion are not only allowed, but are accepted as important.

Content Perspective

Brendan Buckley, a ten-year-old budding scientist interested in geology, unexpectedly encounters the white grandfather he has never known at a rock show. As he struggles with his grandfather's estrangement from the family, he uncovers a painful truth. Frazier confronts the racist hurt sometimes experienced in biracial families. She conveys the importance of family values and community without being heavy-handed or didactic, and she uses the study of science as a metaphor for the process of bringing a disparate family back together.

Discussion Openers

Students should provide examples of text and/or illustrations to support their responses.

- What kind of person is Brendan Buckley?
- Brendan Buckley has two grandparents. In what ways are they different? How are they alike?
- Grandma Gladys always tells the truth. Why is this important in her relationship with Brendan?
- How did using the scientific method help Brendan find his other grandfather?
- This is a book about interracial relationships. Why was this a problem in Brendan Buckley's world?

Beyond the Book

- How does tae kwon do contribute to the concept of diversity in the story?
- Identify a culture that you are not familiar with and compare its celebrations, food, and traditions with your own.
- Interview an adult family member about his or her experiences with another culture.
- How can having a hobby lead to new discoveries?
- President Barack Obama comes from a biracial family much like Brendan's. What role did grandparents play in this president's life?

Books for Further Discussions

Brendan Buckley's Sixth-Grade Experiment by Sundee T. Frazier. Delacorte, 2012. (CSK–John Steptoe Winner)

The Dreamer by Pam Muñoz Ryan. Scholastic, 2010. (Pura Belpre Winner)

One Crazy Summer by Rita Williams-Garcia. HarperCollins/Amistad, 2010. (CSK Winner, Newbery Honor)

The Road to Paris by Nikki Grimes. Putnam, 2006. (CSK Honor)

Brothers in Hope: The Story of the Lost Boys of Sudan

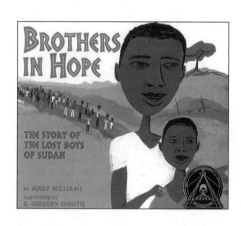

By Mary Williams, illus. by
R. Gregory Christie
N.Y., Lee & Low, 2005
Grade: 3–5
Genre: Historical Fiction/Picture
Book
Core Democratic Value: Common Good
People should work together for the good of all. The government should make laws that are good for everyone.

Content Perspective

Out of a war that claimed the lives of more than two million people comes the story of children now known as the Lost Boys of Sudan. In this fictionalized retelling, first-person narrator Garang reveals how everything changed in the blink of an eye, from secure family life to a life of total chaos. The words of his father, "There is nothing you cannot do," ring in his ears as he and thirty-five boys in his care trek from Sudan to Ethiopia, and on to Kenya, finally finding homes in the United States. Mary Williams tells this amazing story with great sensitivity, including the few players who helped the boys along the way. R. Gregory Christie's illustrations bring Africa to life, from the stark golden desert to the swollen Gilo River. He paints courage and perseverance across every page.

Discussion Openers

Students should provide examples of text and/or illustrations to support their responses.

• What character traits showed that Garang was a responsible member of the Lost Boys?

- Some of the boys were only five years old. What was the first and most important thing all of the boys needed to learn once they realized there was no adult to look after them?
- Give examples of how the Lost Boys worked together toward a common good.
- What was the most difficult aspect of the Lost Boys' journey?
- In addition to the war, what other dangers did the Lost Boys face?

Beyond the Book

- On a world map, calculate the distance from Sudan to Ethiopia and then to Kenya. Imagine walking that distance. Taking into consideration climate and terrain, how long would it take even if you were well prepared?
- Once the Lost Boys arrived in the United States, they faced further challenges. Identify the challenges and make recommendations that might be helpful.
- Using a world map, list the countries that are in Africa.
- Imagine that one of the Lost Boys is a new student at your school. What might you do to make him feel comfortable?
- Choose one of the people that helped the boys and research the person's commitment to them.

Books for Further Discussions

Bird in a Box by Andrea Davis Pinkney, illus. by Sean Qualls. Little, Brown, 2011.

The Crow-Girl: The Children of Crow Cove by Bodil Bredsdorff, translated from the Danish by Faith Ingwersen. Farrar, Straus and Giroux, 2004. (Batchelder Honor)

Locomotion by Jacqueline Woodson. Putnam, 2003. (CSK Honor)

The Orphans of Normandy: A True Story of World War II Told through Drawings by Children by Nancy Amis. Atheneum, 2003.

Christmas in the Big House, Christmas in the Quarters

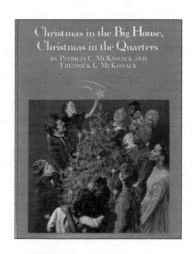

By Patricia C. McKissack and Fredrick L. McKissack, illus. by John Thompson
N.Y., Scholastic, 1994

Grade: 4–6

Genre: Nonfiction

Core Democratic Value: Liberty

Liberty includes the freedom to believe what you want, to choose your own friends, to have your own ideas and opinions, to express your ideas in public, to meet in groups, and to have any lawful job or business.

Content Perspective

Christmas in the Big House, Christmas in the Quarters dramatizes the contradictions of Virginia plantation life in 1859. A clear line is drawn between what happens at Christmastime with the family of the plantation owner and how the holiday plays out for those enslaved on the plantation. The differences are dramatic, but not overplayed. The story focuses on the celebratory nature of the holiday.

Discussion Openers

Students should provide examples of text and/or illustrations to support their responses.

- Who were the "northern meddlers," and why were they so disliked by southern plantation owners?
- Christmastime was "reunion time for families sold away from their loved ones." Why was this a mixed blessing for enslaved people living in the quarters?
- The McKissacks refer to a secret reader who would share Douglass's words about freedom and the abolitionist movement. Why was it risky to be a secret reader?

- Enslaved people recognized the importance of learning to read. Why was it necessary to keep their ability to read a secret?
- How were enslaved people used in the celebration in the Big House? What purpose did they serve for that celebration?

Beyond the Book

- Who was Harriet Tubman, and why was there a reward on her head?
- Read the notes from page 44. Discuss what it might have felt like to be Dangerfield Newby's wife after the Harper's Ferry rebellion.
- Research the lives of Charles Sumner, white abolitionist and U.S. senator from Massachusetts, and Representative Preston Brooks of South Carolina. Compare and contrast their views on slavery.
- Why was it important for those living in the quarters to remember what happened aboard the Creole?
- Langston Hughes lived a long time after slavery. Look at the Langston Hughes poem on page 56 and discuss how this poem bridges the time of slavery to the twentieth century.

Books for Further Discussions

At Her Majesty's Request: An African Princess in Victorian England by Walter Dean Myers, Scholastic, 1999. (Orbis Pictus Honor)

César: Sí, Se Puede!: Yes, We Can! by Carmen T. Bernier-Grand, illus. by David Diaz. Marshall Cavendish, 2004. (Pura Belpre Honor)

The Poet Slave of Cuba: A Biography of Juan Francisco Manzano by Margarita Engle. Henry Holt, 2006. (Pura Belpre Winner)

Rosa by Nikki Giovanni, illus. by Bryan Collier. Henry Holt, 2005. (Caldecott Honor, CSK Winner)

Sit-In: How Four Friends Stood Up by Sitting Down by Andrea Davis Pinkney, illus. by Brian Pinkney. Little, Brown, 2010. (Woodson Winner, Jane Addams Honor)

Circle of Gold

By Candy Dawson Boyd
N.Y., Scholastic, 1984
Grade: 3–5
Genre: Fiction
Core Democratic Value: Common Good
People should work together for the good of all. The government should make laws that are good for everyone.

Content Perspective

Mattie and her twin, Matt, work hard to help their mother manage after their dad passes away. Back then they both felt loved by both parents. Now Mama seems to be always busy, angry, or fussing about something they did or did not do. Mother's Day is coming, however, and Mattie has an idea to make her mother happy. All she needs to do is win the cash prize for writing an essay for the *South Side Daily* and buy her mother a special pin. The problem is that although she is a pretty good student, Mattie doesn't write very well. When Mattie shares her idea with her neighbor and friend, Mrs. Stamps, Mrs. Stamps notes that it sounds like a long shot. Seeing her mother's frustration with money and her constant struggle to find time for the maintenance tasks that allow the family to live in their apartment, Mattie decides to do whatever it takes to buy the gift she is sure will make her mother happy.

Discussion Openers

Students should provide examples of text and/or illustrations to support their responses.

- Describe the progressive nature of the bullying activity in the story and discuss alternate resolutions.
- Mattie and Matt are twins. Discuss evidence of ways they help and support each other.
- Identify events in the story that tell the reader how or what Mrs. Benson feels.

- Which of the following character traits *best* describe Mattie: responsibility, honesty, caring, sharing, respectfulness, belief in the Golden Rule? Explain your choices.
- Describe three of the adults in the story. Discuss the role that each one played in Mattie's life.

Beyond the Book

- What do you think about Mattie's freedom to travel about town to shop, visit friends or play at the local park. What places are you allowed to go alone?
- When is it okay to say no to a friend?
- How does your school address the issue of bullying?
- Research information about twins to find out what you don't know about them.
- Research writing contests for children and identify one that you would like to enter. Share contest rules with your teacher and classmates.

Books for Further Discussions

Jake and Lily by Jerry Spinelli. Balzer & Bray, 2012.

Odd Girl In by Jo Whittemore. Alladin, 2011.

The Other Half of My Heart by Sundee T. Frazier. Delacorte, 2010.

Seven Spools of Thread: A Kwanzaa Story by Angela Shelf Medearis, illus. by Daniel Minter. Albert Whitman, 2000.

Elijah of Buxton

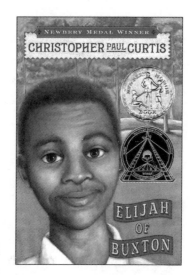

By Christopher Paul Curtis
N.Y., Scholastic, 2007
Grade: 4–6
Genre: Historical Fiction
Core Democratic Value: Rule of Law
*Both the government and the people
must obey the law.*

Content Perspective

The town of Buxton, Canada, was founded
as a safe place where former slaves from
the United States could live in freedom. Eleven-year-old Elijah is very
proud that he is the first free child born in this supportive and caring
community. When his friend's money is stolen, he feels a sense of duty,
in spite of his own fears and the prospect of a dangerous journey, to
retrieve the money. An unforeseen twist of fate finds him face to face
with enslaved Africans, and he must make a difficult choice. In this
coming-of-age story Elijah returns home, no longer a fragile boy but a
brave young man, with an unexpected surprise.

Discussion Openers

Students should provide examples of text and/or illustrations to support
their responses.

- Rules play an important part in maintaining the order of the Buxton
  community. What were some of the rules?
- How did the settlement deal with rule breakers?
- Provide evidence of how Elijah changes so that the term "fragile"
  no longer applies at the end of the story.
- The *n* word is an explosive term. Discuss why Mr. Leroy's reaction
  to Elijah's use of this term is still considered valid today, nearly
  150 years later.
- How does the author use humor to lighten a serious subject?
  Cite examples.

Beyond the Book

- Locate the website for the Buxton National Historic Site & Museum, www.buxtonmuseum.com. Click on Scrapbook. How is the rule of law evident in the establishment of the Buxton settlement?
- Is the concept of respecting your elders a core democratic value? Why or why not?
- Some Buxton residents worked tirelessly to earn enough money to buy the freedom of family members left behind. Imagine a member of your family in slavery. Draw up a plan to purchase or rescue the person. Write the person's story.
- What experiences do you have with rules? What purpose do rules serve?
- When is it okay not to follow rules?

Books for Further Discussions

I, Dred Scott: A Fictional Slave Narrative Based on the Life and Legal Precedent of Dred Scott by Shelia P. Moses. Margaret K. McElderry, 2005.

I Thought My Soul Would Rise and Fly: The Diary of Patsy, a Freed Girl by Joyce Hansen. Scholastic, 1997. (CSK Honor)

Rules by Cynthia Lord. Scholastic 2006. (Schneider Winner, Newbery Honor)

Freedom River

By Doreen Rappaport,
illus. by Bryan Collier
N.Y., Hyperion/Jump at the
Sun, 2000
Grade: 3–5
Genre: Historical Fiction/
Picture Book
Core Democratic Value:
Common Good
Help others.

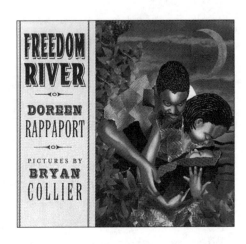

Content Perspective

John Parker, once enslaved, now a business owner, believed strongly in helping others, even if it meant risking his own life. Conducting more than a hundred trips across the Ohio River to rescue runaway slaves, *Freedom River* is about just one of those. Sarah and Isaac are reluctant runaways, and John has to convince them that he would rescue their baby, sleeping at the foot of the Shrofe plantation owner's bed, before they would agree to his escape plan. Bryan Collier's rich illustrations heighten the drama of Rappaport's intense storytelling.

Discussion Openers

Students should provide examples of text and/or illustrations to support their responses.

- What kind of man was Jim Shrofe?
- Why was it so important for John Parker to keep helping others "no matter the risk"?
- Why were Sarah and Isaac reluctant to go along with John Parker's plan?
- What made them finally agree to John Parker's plan?
- Choose one of Bryan Collier's illustrations and create a story for the picture.

Beyond the Book

- What was the purpose of the abolitionist movement?
- Many people, both black and white, were part of the abolitionist movement. Research Frederick Douglass and Harriet Tubman and list their significant contributions to the movement.
- Consult a map of the United States and trace the route that escaped slaves from Kentucky would have traveled in order to reach safety across the Ohio River.
- Learn more about John Parker by going online. List at least three things about him that were not included in *Freedom River*.
- Choose another Coretta Scott King Award–winning picture book and compare the art to that of Bryan Collier in *Freedom River*.

Books for Further Discussions

Freedom School, Yes! by Amy Littlesugar, illus. by Floyd Cooper. Philomel, 2001.

In the Time of the Drums by Kim L. Siegelson, illus. by Brian Pinkney. Hyperion/Jump at the Sun, 1999. (CSK Winner)

Night Boat to Freedom by Margot Theis Raven, illus. by E. B. Lewis. Farrar, Straus and Giroux, 2006. (Jane Addams Honor)

Underground by Shane W. Evans. Roaring Brook, 2011. (CSK Winner)

Freedom Summer

By Deborah Wiles, illus. by Jerome
Lagarrigue
N.Y., Atheneum, 2001
Grade: 3–5
Genre: Historical Fiction/Picture Book
Core Democratic Value: Equality
Give everyone an equal chance.

Content Perspective

During the summer of 1964, the Civil Rights Act became law. *Freedom Summer* is the story of friendship between two young boys, one white and one African American, during that summer. John Henry and Joe enjoy a strong friendship as they spend the long summer days together. When they hear the law has passed they know it opens the town pool "to everybody under the sun, no matter what the color." The next day, they run to the pool, only to find workers filling it with "hot spongy tar." Although the boys realize that it will take more than a law to make some people change, they test a different newfound freedom and go into a store together to buy an ice pop. Jerome Lagarrigue's muted tones quietly evoke the atmosphere of a southern summer and beautifully portray the strong bonds of friendship between John Henry and Joe.

Discussion Openers

Students should provide examples of text and/or illustrations to support their responses.

- Was the opening of the pool more important to John Henry than to Joe? Why or why not?
- How did John Henry feel about having to wait outside while Joe purchased their ice pops?
- Joe refers to Annie Mae by her first name. Do you call adults by their first name? Why or why not?
- Choose one of Lagarrigue's illustrations and create a story for the picture.

- What did Joe mean when he said, "I want to see this town with John Henry's eyes"?

Beyond the Book

- What effect would the closing of a pool have on a community?
- Create a story about how Joe's family would have responded to the closing of the pool.
- Create a list of leaders of the civil rights movement. Identify someone you particularly admire. Write about why you chose this person.
- Interview an adult family member or friend about what he or she knows about the civil rights movement. How would their stories help you better understand *Freedom Summer*?
- Did you ever swim in a community pool? Write and illustrate a story about that experience.

Books for Further Discussions

The Great Migration: Journey to the North by Eloise Greenfield, illus. by Jan Spivey Gilchrist. HarperCollins/Amistad, 2011. (CSK Honor)

A Sweet Smell of Roses by Angela Johnson, illus. by Eric Velasquez. Simon & Schuster, 2005.

We March by Shane W. Evans. Roaring Brook, 2012.

The Friendship

By Mildred D. Taylor, illus. by
Max Ginsburg
N.Y., Dial, 1987
Grade: 4–6
Genre: Historical Fiction
Core Democratic Value: Equality
*Everyone should get the same treatment,
regardless of race, religion, economic status,
or where one's parents or grandparents were
born.*

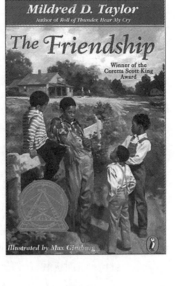

Content Perspective

Aunt Callie sends Cassie Logan and her brothers on a dangerous mission. It is Mississippi in the 1930s and the mission is to pick up headache medicine for their elderly neighbor. The problem is this. The store, owned by Mr. John Wallace, has been off-limits for the Logan children because everyone knows that Jim Crow laws are practiced there, particularly the law about how blacks must address whites. The children are careful, but old Mr. Tom Bee is not. He enters the store and calls the owner by his given name, John. The children witness this tragic confrontation that further drives home the terror under which the black community lives. Some racist words are used. However, within this context they are necessary and provide opportunities for a serious discussion of language and its relationship to racism and equality.

Discussion Openers

Students should provide examples of text and/or illustrations to support their responses.

- Keeping in mind the core democratic value of equality, list the ways that Jim Crow laws limited the life of the Logan children.
- Why did Mr. Tom Bee ask the children to wait for him while he was in the store?

- What example did Mr. Tom Bee set for the children? Do you think it was intentional?
- Was it right for Mr. Tom Bee to call Mr. John Wallace by his first name? Why or why not?
- Would you like to have a friend like Mr. John Wallace? Why or why not?

Beyond the Book

- Visit this PBS website: www.pbs.org/wnet/jimcrow/stories.html and select Personal Narratives. Click on one of the people listed and listen to his or her story. How do you think it would feel to be that person?
- Research author Mildred D. Taylor. Write a brief essay about what inspired her writing.
- Interview an adult relative about what it was like when he or she was growing up. How is it similar to your experience? How is it different?
- Go online and find a list of Jim Crow laws for a state near you. Discuss the implications of such laws.
- How does the Logan children's experience relate to bullying? Why is bullying always wrong?

Books for Further Discussions

Claudette Colvin : Twice Toward Justice by Phillip Hoose. Farrar/Kroupa, 2009. (Newbery Honor, Sibert Honor, Woodson Winner)

One Crazy Summer by Rita Williams-Garcia. HarperCollins/Amistad, 2010. (CSK Winner, Newbery Honor)

Sit-In: How Four Friends Stood Up by Sitting Down by Andrea Davis Pinkney, illus. by Brian Pinkney. Little, Brown, 2010. (Jane Addams Honor, Woodson Winner)

We Troubled the Waters by Ntozake Shange, illus. by Rod Brown. Harper-Collins/Amistad, 2009.

I Have Heard of a Land

By Joyce Carol Thomas,
illus. by Floyd Cooper
N.Y., HarperCollins, 1998
Grade: 3–6
Genre: Historical Fiction/Picture Book
Core Democratic Value: Common Good
People should work together for the good of all. The government should make laws that are good for everyone.

Content Perspective

The Oklahoma Territory of the late 1800s offered those with the courage to act an opportunity for free land. With lyrical language, Joyce Carol Thomas captures the riveting story of one woman brave enough to join the land run and stake a claim in this vast and unknown territory. The narrative sings with the joy of knowing that land ownership means real freedom. Floyd Cooper's honey-hued illustrations exude the confidence and determination of these extraordinary pioneers.

Discussion Openers

Students should provide examples of text and/or illustrations to support their responses.

- Why is *I Have Heard of a Land* a good example of common good as a core democratic value?
- Which illustration best demonstrates the core democratic value of common good? Explain.
- What is the meaning of the line, "Where what is dreamed one night / Is accomplished the next day"?
- There are many examples of metaphorical language in *I Have Heard of a Land*. Discuss how it is used.
- The illustrations have a dreamlike quality to them. Who is telling the story?

Beyond the Book

- There are many perspectives from which to view the Oklahoma land run. Visit www.okhistory.org/kids/lrexhibit and explore the various perspectives.
- Based on the information provided at the above website, whose perspective was excluded from the core democratic value of common good? Explain.
- The concept of a land run is still in existence today. Search online for examples and explain how they are similar yet different from the land run of the 1800s.
- Today, people run for a variety of causes such as breast cancer, muscular dystrophy, or sometimes to raise money for a local school. Explore options for running for a cause and share that information with your classmates.
- Running is a healthy form of exercise. Time how many minutes you run each day and try to increase the amount of time you spend running.

Books for Further Discussions

One Crazy Summer by Rita Williams-Garcia. HarperCollins/Amistad, 2010. (CSK Winner, Newbery Honor)

Rosa by Nikki Giovanni, illus. by Bryan Collier. Henry Holt, 2005. (Caldecott Honor, CSK Winner)

Sit-In: How Four Friends Stood Up by Sitting Down by Andrea Davis Pinkney, illus. by Brian Pinkney. Little, Brown, 2010. (Jane Addams Honor, Woodson Winner)

Jazz

By Walter Dean Myers,
illus. by Christopher Myers
N.Y., Holiday House, 2006
Grade: 3–6
Genre: Historical Fiction/Picture Book
Core Democratic Value: Diversity
*Differences in language, dress, food,
music, the place where parents or grandparents were born, race, and religion
are not only allowed, but are accepted as
important.*

Content Perspective

Bold dramatic paintings by Christopher Myers celebrate the different styles of jazz. Author Walter Dean Myers's poems offer a tribute to this original American musical genre. An introduction to jazz at the beginning of the book and a useful timeline and glossary at the end add authenticity and historical relevance to this musical tribute.

Discussion Openers

Students should provide examples of text and/or illustrations to support their responses.

- What was the author's purpose in writing this book?
- Identify words or phrases in two different poems that suggest feelings.
- Think about the musicians pictured with their eyes closed. What message do those illustrations send to the reader?
- Which of the five senses do you experience when you look at the illustrations for "Blue Creeps In," and "Three Voices"?
- Read the first page of the introduction. Share with your classmates three facts about jazz that you found interesting.

Beyond the Book

- Look up the dictionary meaning of the following terms from the Glossary of Jazz Terms at the end of the book: *ballad*, *chops*, *fusion*, *hip*.
- Choose one of the jazz artists mentioned in the timeline at the end of the book and research his or her musical contributions. Share your findings with your classmates.
- Music often elicits an emotional response. Listen to a selection by one of the musicians listed in the timeline. What emotions are evoked when you hear this music?
- Charlie Parker and Dizzy Gillespie are considered cofounders of bebop. What is bebop and how does it differ from other forms of jazz?
- Identify five instruments frequently found in jazz ensembles.

Books for Further Discussions

Aida by Leontyne Price, illus. by Leo and Diane Dillon. Harcourt, 1990. (CSK Winner)

Jazz on a Saturday Night by Leo and Diane Dillon. Scholastic/Blue Sky, 2007. (CSK Honor)

Rap a Tap Tap: Here's Bojangles—Think of That! by Leo and Diane Dillon. Scholastic, 2002. (CSK Honor)

Ray Charles by Sharon Bell Mathis, illus. by George Ford. Lee & Low, 2001. (CSK Winner)

Justin and the Best Biscuits in the World

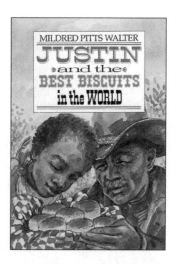

By Mildred Pitts Walter,
illus by Catherine Stock
N.Y., Lothrop, Lee and Shepard, 1986
Grade: 3–5
Genre: Fiction
Core Democratic Value: Common Good
Help others at home and at school.

Content Perspective

Ten-year-old Justin must cope with being the sole male in the house after his father dies. Much to the dismay of his sisters and sometimes his mother, Justin thinks that chores like making his bed or washing the dishes are "women's work." Justin regularly frustrates his sisters as he bungles most of the chores he is asked to do. As a result, he is often grounded until he completes his jobs. When Justin gets a chance to visit his grandfather, he learns the proud history of the black cowboys of the old West. Grandfather also shares the history of his own family and the importance of knowing the family legacy. During his stay, Justin gets a fresh perspective on the household chores that were such a frustration at home. He learns that a man can complete those same chores with the pride of accomplishment.

Discussion Openers

Students should provide examples of text and/or illustrations to support their responses.

- Do you know how to make a bed with no lumps, bumps, or wrinkles?
- What did Grandfather mean by his statement: "The brave hide their fears, but share their tears. Tears bathe the soul."
- Have you ever entered a contest at a festival or fair? If so, what competitions did you compete in? If not, what competitions do you believe you would you be best at?

- What surprised you most after reading excerpts of the diary of Grandpa's great-grandpa, *Reflections on My Young Life,* by Phillip Ward, Sr.?
- Discuss Justin's progression from viewing making his bed and washing the dishes as women's work to becoming skilled at completing household tasks.
- Outline the motivation and progression of Grandpa's forebears in their quest to move to Missouri, highlight the challenges they faced.

Beyond the Book

- Research one of the black cowboys mentioned in the text. Share your findings with your classmates.
- Outline the motivation and progression of Grandpa's forebears in their quest to move to Missouri. Highlight the challenges they faced.
- Share three things about your own family history with your classmates.
- Discuss the roles of adult males and adult females with your classmates. Make a chart outlining exclusive and shared roles.
- Have you ever visited a ranch? List the differences between living on a ranch and living in the city.

Books for Further Discussions

Bird in a Box by Andrea Davis Pinkney. Little, Brown, 2011.

Brothers in Hope by Mary Williams, illus. by R. Gregory Christie. Lee & Low, 2005. (CSK Honor)

Bud, Not Buddy by Christopher Paul Curtis. Delacorte, 1999. (CSK Winner, Newbery Winner).

Circle of Gold by Candy Dawson Boyd. Scholastic, 1984. (CSK Honor)

One Crazy Summer by Rita Williams-Garcia. HarperCollins/Amistad, 2010. (CSK Winner, Newbery Honor)

Let It Shine: Stories of Black Women Freedom Fighters

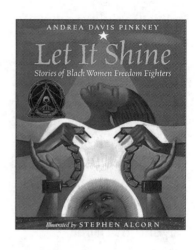

By Andrea Davis Pinkney,
illus. by Stephen Alcorn
N.Y., Harcourt, 2000
Grade: 4–6
Genre: Biography
Core Democratic Value: Justice

All people should be treated fairly in getting the advantages and disadvantages of our country. No group or person should be favored.

Content Perspective

Author Andrea Davis Pinkney presents portraits of women whose fight for freedom covered a range of oppressions. Her subjects include familiar and lesser-known figures. Readers will learn the stories of heroines such as Biddy Mason, Dorothy Height, and Fanny Lou Hamer, along with the more familiar Ella Josephine Baker, Shirley Chisholm, and Rosa Parks. Each of these brave and determined women acted to improve the world for others while addressing the frustrations in her own life. Authentic details, colorful language, and powerful imagery will engage and inspire the reader.

Discussion Openers

Students should provide examples of text and/or illustrations to support their responses.

- Beyond being black and female, what did each of the women have in common?
- Most of the women in the book did hard, backbreaking work at one time or another. How did these experiences affect their life choices?
- Several of the women in these stories were separated from their parents by the circumstances of the times. Choose three women and discuss the impact of these separations on their chosen paths.

- What role did teachers play in the lives of the women in these stories? Choose three heroines and discuss the influence of teachers in their early education.
- Excluding those quotations located at the beginning of each chapter, create your own quotable quotes based on these stories.

Beyond the Book

- Make a list of organizations, associations, and groups that helped or hindered the women freedom fighters early on in their lives. Research and report on their current operational status, purposes, and goals.
- All of the women received financial support at some point in her struggles. Is it possible they might never have achieved greatness without it? Why or why not?
- In what ways did failure affect the lives of these women? Describe the sequence of events following an apparent failure in the life or career of one of the women in the book.
- Look up the definition of *selfless*. Identify someone in your life who fits this definition.
- Select your favorite Mary McLeod Bethune quote from the following website and share it with your classmates: http://africanamerican quotes.org/mary-mcleod-bethune.html.

Books for Further Discussions

Claudette Colvin: Twice Toward Justice by Phillip Hoose. Farrar/Kroupa, 2009. (Newbery Honor, Sibert Honor, Woodson Winner, Jane Addams Honor)

Talkin' About Bessie: The Story of Aviator Elizabeth Coleman by Nikki Grimes. Orchard, 2002. (CSK Honor/Winner)

A Thousand Never Evers by Shana Burg. Delacorte, 2008.

Locomotion

By Jacqueline Woodson
N.Y., Putnam, 2003
Grade: 4–6
Genre: Poetry
Core Democratic Value:
Pursuit of Happiness
All people can find happiness in their own way,
as long as they do not step on the rights of
others.

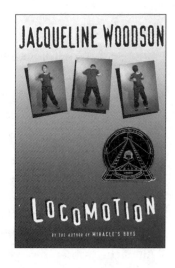

Content Perspective

"This whole book's a poem because poetry's short and / this whole book's a poem 'cause Ms. Marcus says / write it down before it leaves your brain." And Lonnie Collins does just that in Jacqueline Woodson's poetic novel *Locomotion*. Sixty carefully crafted poems reveal the events and people in Lonnie's life: the fire that killed his parents; his foster mother; and his efforts to maintain a relationship with his adopted younger sister, Lili.

Discussion Openers

Students should provide examples of text and/or illustrations to support their responses.

- *Locomotion* tells us a lot about the people in Lonnie's life. What kind of person is Ms. Edna?
- What effect did Ms. Edna have on Lonnie's ability to pursue personal happiness?
- Lonnie wrote a "List Poem" on page 33. Reread the poem and discuss why he wrote it. Write your own list poem, and discuss why you chose to write it the way you did.
- Reread Lonnie's description of a new boy in school. Have you ever been the new kid? Have you ever made friends with a new kid? Write a poem about how it might feel to be the new kid.
- How does Lonnie feel about his sister, Lili? How does Lili feel about her brother?

- How did Lonnie feel when he first saw the pictures of Ms. Edna's sons? Did his thinking change after he met one of them?
- Why was Lonnie unable to tell his story in the order that it happened?

Beyond the Book

- Lonnie is named after the song "The Locomotion" by Little Eva. Choose a song that says who you are.
- Listen to "The Locomotion" by Little Eva and list words that most closely describe Lonnie.
- Woodson's poems explain how Lonnie got his name. Interview a relative and ask how that person got his or her name. Write a poem to explain the story behind the name.
- Reread the poem "Telling Tales." Write a poem about your wildest dreams and discuss how you might achieve them.
- The pursuit of happiness means different things to different people. Explain what it means to you.

Books for Further Discussions

Money Hungry by Sharon G. Flake. Hyperion, 2001. (CSK Honor)

The Red Rose Box by Brenda Woods. Putnam, 2002. (CSK Honor)

The Road to Paris by Nikki Grimes. Putnam, 2006. (CSK Honor)

Stitches by Glen Huser. Groundwood, 2003.

The Way a Door Closes by Hope Anita Smith, illus. by Shane W. Evans. Henry Holt, 2003. (CSK–John Steptoe Winner)

Never Forgotten

By Patricia C. McKissack,
illus. by Leo and Diane Dillon
N.Y., Swartz & Wade, 2011

Grade: 3–5

Genre: Folklore

Core Democratic Value:
Pursuit of Happiness
All people can find happiness in their
own way, as long as they do not step
on the rights of others.

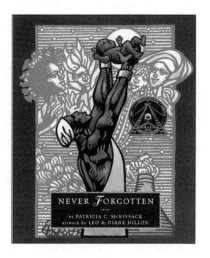

Content Perspective

A beautiful collaboration of the Dillon illustrator team and Patricia C. McKissack, this book tells the story of a blacksmith's, son, Musafa, who was taken captive and sold into slavery across the sea. The story recounts the misery of father, Dinga, along with the elements, Earth, Fire, Water, and Wind, whose power is not enough to bring Musafa home. It is a reminder to all that the loss of a child can never be forgotten.

Discussion Openers

Students should provide examples of text and/or illustrations to support their responses.

- What evidence do you have that Dinga was a devoted father?
- Reread the saying that Dinga taught Musafa. Discuss ways it has meaning in today's world.
- What were the Mother Elements? What roles did they play in the story?
- Musafa was a very special person. Think about his character and how his upbringing worked in his favor as an enslaved person.
- Read the last three lines of the poem "Beware." What does the poem tell you about paying attention?

Beyond the Book

- Design a metal item of your own (garden element, banister, fence gate, etc.).
- Make a chart depicting the elements. How do they affect your life today?
- Research naming ceremonies in African and other indigenous cultures. Share your findings with your classmates.
- Research the iron gates of South Carolina. Share your findings with your classmates.
- Locate three additional titles illustrated by Leo and Diane Dillon. Discuss similarities and differences in their artwork.

Books for Further Discussions

Almost to Freedom by Vaunda Micheaux Nelson, illus. by Colin Bootman. Carolrhoda, 2003. (CSK Honor)

Brothers in Hope: The Story of the Lost Boys of Sudan by Mary Williams, illus. by R. Gregory Christie. Lee & Low, 2007. (CSK Honor)

The People Could Fly: American Black Folktales by Virginia Hamilton, illus. by Leo and Diane Dillon. Knopf, 1985. (CSK Winner/Honor)

The People Could Fly: The Picture Book

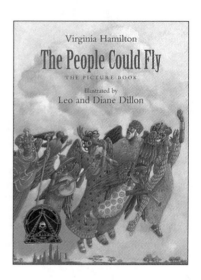

By Virginia Hamilton,
illus. by Leo and Diane Dillon
N.Y., Knopf, 2004

Grade: 4–6

Genre: Folklore

Core Democratic Value: Justice

All people should be treated fairly in getting the advantages and disadvantages of our country. No group or person should be favored.

Content Perspective

Leo and Diane Dillon brilliantly bring to life what might be Virginia Hamilton's finest story, *The People Could Fly: The Picture Book.* This powerful black folktale creates an illusion of hope for the enslaved people left behind, encouraging them to look up and create imaginative schemes that will bring them to freedom. This folktale encapsulates both the harshness and sadness of slavery while portraying a determined desire by the people for justice and freedom.

Discussion Openers

Students should provide examples of text and/or illustrations to support their responses.

- What effect might hearing this story have had on enslaved people?
- Why were enslaved Africans treated so badly?
- What effect might the magic words have had on the enslaved people left behind?
- Why were the lives of enslaved people not protected under the law?
- Choose an illustration from *The People Could Fly: The Picture Book* and create your own story about it.

Beyond the Book

- Did you ever dream that you could fly? Where would you go?
- Research other African folktales about flying. Choose one and compare it to *The People Could Fly: The Picture Book*.
- *Tar Beach* by Faith Ringgold is another picture book about flying. How is it similar to *The People Could Fly: The Picture Book?*
- Why would the idea of flying appeal to someone who is enslaved?
- Superheroes often have the ability to fly. Create and illustrate your own superhero story.

Books for Further Discussions

Further Tales of Uncle Remus: The Misadventures of Brer Rabbit, Brer Fox, Brer Wolf, The Doodang, and Other Creatures told by Julius Lester, illus. by Jerry Pinkney. Dial, 1990.

Her Stories: African American Folktales, Fairy Tales, and True Tales told by Virginia Hamilton, illus. by Leo and Diane Dillon. Blue Sky, 1995. (CSK Winner)

In the Time of the Drums by Kim L. Siegelson, illus. by Brian Pinkney. Hyperion/Jump at the Sun, 1999. (CSK Winner)

Tar Beach by Faith Ringgold. Crown, 1991. (CSK Winner, Caldecott Honor)

When Birds Could Talk & Bats Could Sing: The Adventures of Bruh Sparrow, Sis Wren, and Their Friends told by Virginia Hamilton, illus. by Barry Moser. Blue Sky, 1996.

The Red Rose Box

By Brenda Woods
N.Y., Putnam, 2002
Grade: 4–6
Genre: Fiction
Core Democratic Value: Equality
Everyone should get the same treatment, regardless of race, religion, economic status, or where one's parents or grandparents were born.

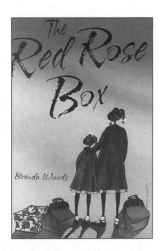

Content Perspective

The Red Rose Box is a deceptively simple coming-of-age tale of two young girls growing up between two worlds: the Jim Crow cotton fields of Sulphur, Louisiana, and the desegregated neighborhoods of Los Angeles in the 1950s. Brenda Woods unveils the promise and hope of ten-year-old Leah and her sister Ruth on their journey with Leah's red rose traveling case. Woods vividly portrays the young protagonists' internal and external struggle for a sense of place and belonging.

Discussion Openers

Students should provide examples of text and/or illustrations to support their responses.

- Los Angeles is very different from rural Louisiana. Explain some of the differences.
- When Leah, Ruth, Micah, and Nathan encountered two white men while walking on the road, how did the children respond? Why?
- Mama, Gramma, and the two girls stepped into "the colored section on that Jim Crow train." What is a Jim Crow train?
- After the tragic hurricane claimed the lives of Leah's and Ruth's parents, the girls moved to Los Angeles with Aunt Olivia. When she took them to the library, why did Leah want to choose sad books?
- Compare the characters of Leah and Ruth. How are they different? How are they the same?

Beyond the Book

- If you could create your own personal red rose box, what would you put in it? Justify your choices.
- Interview a close adult relative. Ask about Jim Crow laws. How does your relative's account compare with those in *The Red Rose Box*?
- Research Jim Crow laws and explain how they might have affected the lives of Leah and Ruth.
- Who were the Pullman porters? What role did they play in the civil rights movement?
- During the 1940s and 1950s the train called the Super Chief was unique in many ways. What made the Super Chief different from other passenger trains?

Books for Further Discussions

As Good As Anybody: Martin Luther King, Jr. and Abraham Joshua Heschel's Amazing March Toward Freedom by Richard Michelson, illus. by Raúl Colón. Knopf, 2008. (Sydney Taylor Winner)

Brendan Buckley's Universe and Everything in It by Sundee T. Frazier. Delacorte, 2007. (CSK–John Steptoe Winner)

Elijah of Buxton by Christopher Paul Curtis. Scholastic, 2007. (CSK Winner, Newbery Honor, Jane Addams Honor)

Now Is Your Time! The African-American Struggle for Freedom by Walter Dean Myers. Scholastic, 1991. (CSK Winner, Woodson Honor, Jane Addams Honor, Orbis Pictus Honor)

Sonia Sotomayor: First Hispanic U.S. Supreme Court Justice by Lisa Tucker McElroy. Lerner, 2010.

The Tales of Uncle Remus: The Adventures of Brer Rabbit

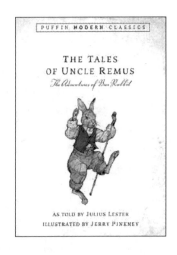

Told by Julius Lester,
illus. by Jerry Pinkney
N.Y., Dial, 1987
Grade: 3–6
Genre: Folklore
Core Democratic Value: Pursuit of Happiness
All people can find happiness in their own way, as long as they do not step on the rights of others.

Content Perspective

Author Julius Lester skillfully injects his storyteller voice into each tale in ways that make the stories relevant and current to today's reader. His ability to make a talking rabbit visiting a shopping mall believable is incredible. He covers any disbelief readers might have by reminding them that "this is a tale told to him." The fact that the rabbit considers himself to be both slippery and smart reminds readers that not thinking can easily get you into trouble, while thinking ahead can keep you out of trouble.

Discussion Openers

Students should provide examples of text and/or illustrations to support their responses.

- Make a list of sayings that you enjoyed from the book: e.g., "like wet on water," or "that's the way the rain falls."
- Of all the female characters in the stories (designated as Sister or Miz), which ones came closest to outwitting Brer Rabbit?
- Brer Rabbit regularly displayed people smarts or book learning to outwit the other animals. Find a story that demonstrates this.

- Some of the stories have an abrupt ending, or an ending without resolution. Why do you believe author Julius Lester used this strategy?
- Create your own illustration for one of the stories.
- Retell one of the stories from the point of view of a character other than Brer Rabbit.

Beyond the Book

- Read the introduction by Augusta Baker and discuss the three ingredients of language used in the telling of the Brer Rabbit stories.
- The Brer Rabbit stories are cultural tales. Identify other collections of tales specific to different cultures.
- Research the history of Uncle Remus as a teller of tales.
- Read Ashley Bryan's African folktale "The Lion and the Ostrich Chicks." Discuss the similarities and differences between Bryan's writing and Lester's writing.
- What messages could *The Tales of Uncle Remus* have for modern-day youth?

Books for Further Discussions

Claudette Colvin: Twice Toward Justice by Phillip Hoose. Farrar/Kroupa, 2009. (Newbery Honor, Sibert Honor, Jane Addams Honor, Woodson Winner)

The Dreamer by Pam Muñoz Ryan, illus. by Peter Sis. Scholastic, 2010. (Pura Belpre Winner)

Money Hungry by Sharon Flake, Hyperion/Jump at the Sun, 2001. (CSK Honor)

We Troubled the Waters by Ntozake Shange, illus. by Rod Brown. HarperCollins/Amistad, 2009.

CHAPTER 4

Grades 4–8

Black Diamond: The Story of the Negro Baseball Leagues

By Patricia C. McKissack
and Fredrick McKissack Jr.
N.Y., Scholastic, 1994

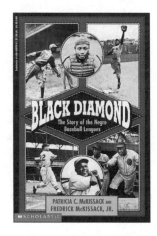

Grade: 5–8

Genre: Nonfiction

Core Democratic Value: Justice

All people should be treated fairly in getting the advantages and disadvantages of our country. No group or person should be favored.

Content Perspective

The story of the Negro Leagues of baseball reveals details about the evolution of the leagues' organizational structure, individual Negro players, and the role of those players in the history of the game. Carefully researched, *Black Diamond* documents the previously overlooked and undervalued historical role of the Negro Leagues in the overall history of baseball in the United States. The stalwart and determined ballplayers suffered from a lack of facilities on the road and inequities in financial remuneration. Included also is the story of the Cuban Giants (1887), the first professional all-black team that played against white teams.

Discussion Openers

Students should provide examples of text and/or illustrations to support their responses.

- What ideas did the baseball industry use to justify not allowing black players to play in the national leagues?
- Do you think it was a good, bad, right, or wrong idea for black players to pretend to be Cuban or Native American in order to play on white teams?
- What effect did the end of World War II have on the ban against Negro players in national baseball leagues?
- Nicknames were reflective of the character, physical prowess, and skill of the players. How did this practice impact the popularity of the Negro Leagues?
- Discuss the hardships imposed on Negro League players.
- What impact did Rube Foster have on the organization of the Negro Leagues?

Beyond the Book

- Choose three players who were not selected for the major leagues who should have been. Support your choice.
- Who was Effa Manley? Why was she important to the progress of Negro League playing conditions?
- Research Negro League baseball in Toledo, Ohio.
- Locate pictures or descriptions of baseball uniforms in the 1930s, 1940s, 1950s, and modern-day uniforms from the 2000s. Discuss changes over time.
- Research prominent Puerto Rican baseball players who played on American teams in the period between 1930 and 1960.

Books for Further Discussions

The Berlin Boxing Club by Robert Sharenow. HarperTeen, 2011. (Sydney Taylor Award Winner)

Heart and Soul: The Story of America and African Americans by Kadir Nelson. Balzer & Bray, 2011. (CSK Winner/Honor, Jane Addams Honor, Orbis Pictus Recommended)

Twelve Rounds to Glory: The Story of Muhammad Ali by Charles R. Smith, Jr., illus. by Bryan Collier. Candlewick, 2007. (CSK Honor)

We Are the Ship: The Story of Negro League Baseball by Kadir Nelson. Hyperion/Jump at the Sun, 2008. (CSK Winner/Honor, Orbis Pictus Honor, Sibert Winner)

Bud, Not Buddy

By Christopher Paul Curtis
N.Y., Delacorte, 1999
Grade: 4–8
Genre: Historical Fiction
Core Democratic Value:
Pursuit of Happiness
It is the right of citizens in the United States to pursue happiness in their own way, as long as they do not infringe upon the rights of others.

Content Perspective

Bud is just ten years old, but he has a plan as he escapes from a cruel foster home in Flint, Michigan. It is 1936, and the country moans with the weight of the Great Depression. Bud is on the run, convinced his father is the famous musician, Herman E. Calloway. He knows a couple of facts about his supposed father; Calloway's band is called the Dusky Devastators of the Depression, and he lives in Grand Rapids, Michigan. Bud has posters left by his deceased mother to prove it. However, getting to Grand Rapids during these turbulent times proves to be more daunting than Bud expected. His determination and the help of caring strangers see him through with a surprising twist at the end.

Discussion Openers

Students should provide examples of text and/or illustrations to support their responses.

- Bud was on the run, and he was hungry. When he arrived at the food line, he was too late—the line had just closed. A family with two young children pulled him into the line, and the parents proceeded to hit him on the side his head several times. What made them do this?
- Why did Bud create a set of rules for himself?
- What evidence can you provide that Bud gave serious thought to how he would get his revenge on the Amoses? How did it make him feel?

- Why was Bud's suitcase so important to him?
- Why was Lefty Lewis an important character in this story? What role did he play in Bud's pursuit of happiness?
- Why did Bud lie to Lefty Lewis about where he came from? Is it ever okay to tell a lie?

Beyond the Book

- Rule number 328 states: "When You Make Up Your Mind to Do Something, Hurry Up and Do It, If You Wait You Might Talk Yourself Out of What You Wanted in the First Place." Explain how this rule might work in your life.
- Bud's favorite saying was: "He who laughs last laughs best." What does that saying mean? Can you give an example of this from your own life?
- The Brotherhood of Pullman Porters was a real organization. Research online what made it so important to the civil rights movement. Why was it dangerous for Pullman porters to form a union?
- Go online to find out more about the Flint sit-down strike of 1936–1937. Write a short essay about what you discover.
- List three things that are essential to your own pursuit of happiness. Explain why they are important.

Books for Further Discussions

Bird in a Box by Andrea Davis Pinkney, illus. by Sean Qualls. Little, Brown, 2011.

Brendan Buckley's Universe and Everything in It by Sundee T. Frasier. Delacorte, 2007. (CSK–John Steptoe Winner)

The Road to Paris by Nikki Grimes. Putnam, 2006. (CSK Honor)

Standing Against the Wind by Traci L. Jones. Farrar, Straus and Giroux, 2006. (CSK–John Steptoe Winner)

Her Stories: African American Folktales, Fairy Tales, and True Tales

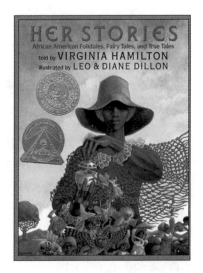

Told by Virginia Hamilton,
illus. by Leo and Diane Dillon
N.Y., Blue Sky, 1995
Grade: 5–9
Genre: Folktale
Core Democratic Value: Diversity
Differences in language, dress, food, race, and religion are not only allowed, but are accepted as important.

Content Perspective

Traditional tales told by and about female heroines are divided into sections covering animal tales, tales of the supernatural, folkways and legends, and true tales. Hamilton draws upon her personal experience as a child listening to stories told by her grandmother, aunts, and elder cousins. Hamilton captures the nuances of voice, time, and place. Of great value are the commentaries by Hamilton that illuminate each tale.

Discussion Openers

Students should provide examples of text and/or illustrations to support their responses.

- Compare the character and powers of the Boo hag, Cat woman, and the Mer-woman.
- Write a character study of Annie Christmas, as depicted in the story of that title.
- Reread the author's note to the reader; then make your own case for a book devoted exclusively to female heroines (and villains too).
- In the story titled "Miz Hattie Gets Some Company," Miz Hattie declares she is as "lonesome as a biscuit without some gravy." Make

a list of similar descriptive phrases from this and other stories in the book.

• How many phrases can you find that depict a time long past (e.g., "long ago") in *Her Stories*?

Beyond the Book

• Reread the story of *Catskinella*. Locate two additional *Cinderella* stories. Discuss the similarities and differences between the stories.
• Discuss the use of colloquial speech or so-called black plantation English in folktales.
• Hamilton's commentary on the story "The Little Girl and Buh Rabby" notes that during plantation times slaves identified readily with small defenseless animals and celebrated their ability to evade capture and punishment. Discuss reasons why this was true.
• Discuss the difference between folktales and fairy tales.
• Make a list of folktales about female characters in different cultures. Label your list by cultures.

Books for Further Discussions

Barbara Jordan by James Haskins. Dial, 1977. (CSK Honor)

The Days When Animals Talked: Black American Folktales and How They Came to Be by William J. Faulkner. Follett, 1977. (CSK Honor)

The Skin I'm In by Sharon G. Flake. Hyperion/Jump at the Sun, 1988. (CSK–John Steptoe Winner)

I Thought My Soul Would Rise and Fly: The Diary of Patsy, a Freed Girl

By Joyce Hansen
N.Y., Scholastic, 1997
Grade: 4–8
Genre: Historical Fiction
Core Democratic Value: Justice
All people should be treated fairly in getting the advantages and disadvantages of our country. No group or person should be favored.

Content Perspective

As part of the Dear America series, *I Thought My Soul Would Rise and Fly* tells the story of Patsy, a young formerly enslaved girl with many strikes against her, who finds herself caught up in the period of Reconstruction. She is exceptional in that she can read and write. Although free, Patsy is chained to the plantation by circumstances beyond her control. Meanwhile, she uses her literary skills to advance her own desire for freedom and justice while acting as teacher for those left on the plantation. As more and more freed people leave, Patsy's responsibilities increase, and she begins to realize just how many talents she has that would serve her well as a free person. Joyce Hansen brings to life the struggles that came with Reconstruction and anchors her work soundly in history with real events, laws, and institutions.

Discussion Openers

Students should provide examples of text and/or illustrations to support their responses.

- How did life for formerly enslaved people change following emancipation? How did it remain the same?
- During Reconstruction, what attempts were made to provide justice for all?

- Why didn't Patsy want other freed people to know she could read and write?
- What made the period of Reconstruction dangerous for formerly enslaved people?
- Was it right for Nancy to stay with Mrs. Davis when her own mother came for her? Why or why not?

Beyond the Book

- Research the Black Codes. How did they prevent newly freed people from achieving justice?
- What purpose did Union Leagues serve during Reconstruction? How did they lead to changes in voting laws?
- Henry McNeal Turner was a minister and later a bishop in the African Methodist Episcopal Church. He was also a member of the first group of blacks to be elected to public office. What role did he play in trying to achieve justice for all African Americans?
- Several times throughout the story, Patsy says, "I thought my soul would rise and fly." Read Virginia Hamilton's *The People Could Fly: The Picture Book* (illustrated by Leo and Diane Dillon) and discuss what effects knowledge of this folktale might have had on enslaved people.
- Create and illustrate a story about what you would do if you could fly.

Books for Further Discussions

Birmingham, 1963 by Carole Boston Weatherford. Wordsong, 2007. (Jane Addams Honor)

Days of Jubilee: The End of Slavery in the United States by Patricia C. and Fredrick L. McKissack. Scholastic, 2003. (CSK Honor)

M.L.K.: Journey of a King by Tonya Bolden, photo. ed. Bob Adelman. Abrams, 2006. (Orbis Pictus Winner)

Thurgood Marshall: A Life for Justice by James Haskins. Henry Holt, 1992. (Woodson Outstanding Merit)

The Voice That Challenged a Nation: Marian Anderson and the Struggle for Equal Rights by Russell Freedman. Clarion, 2004. (Woodson Winner, Sibert Winner, Newbery Honor, Orbis Pictus Honor)

Keeping the Night Watch

By Hope Anita Smith,
illus. by E. B. Lewis
N.Y., Henry Holt, 2008

Grade: 4–6

Genre: Contemporary Realistic
Fiction/Poetry

Core Democratic Value:
Pursuit of Happiness
*All people can find happiness in their own
way, as long as they do not step on the
rights of others.*

Content Perspective

In this continuation of the story that began in *The Way a Door Closes,*
thirteen-year-old C. J. Washington III is having a difficult time after his
father returns from an unexplained absence and reclaims his place in
the family. A series of poems, most in C.J.'s earnest, intelligent voice,
chronicles the path from abandonment to forgiveness. The first-person
account gives readers an intimate view of C.J.'s confusing mix of feelings
toward his father. Using references to scripture and hymns, Smith plays
with a variety of poetic forms, from free verse to shape poems and acros-
tics to sonnets, in a portrait of one family's struggle toward happiness.

Discussion Openers

Students should provide examples of text and/or illustrations to support
their responses.

- C.J. can think of many things that would make him happy: basketball
  camp, his own room with TV and phone, the return of his father. Why
  did Grandmomma warn, "Be careful what you wish for"?
- How do you know that Zuri is afraid? What is she afraid of?
- Why does Zuri name her pillow dog Stay?

- What is C.J. most afraid of when his father returns?
- Compare the illustration of the family on page 2 with the one on the last page of the book. How does illustrator Lewis show the family's changing emotions in the story?
- What does *Keeping the Night Watch* tell us about the pursuit of happiness?

Beyond the Book

- In the poem "Seven Ways of Looking at My Father," C.J. speaks metaphorically about his father. Write seven ways of looking metaphorically at your school.
- Smith uses the shape of a diamond in her poem "The Jeweler." Count syllables and words to see how she constructed this concrete poem. Write your own concrete poem.
- Have you ever gotten something you wished for and later found that it didn't make you happy? Explain.
- Have you ever laid awake at night in anticipation of a coming event? Write a poem about what that might feel like.
- Poetry can present new ways to view the world. Choose a poet whose work you have read and create a biographical sketch of her or his life.

Books for Further Discussions

The Journey Home by Isabelle Holland. Scholastic, 1990.

Locomotion by Jacqueline Woodson. Putnam, 2003. (CSK Honor)

Money Hungry by Sharon G. Flake. Hyperion/Jump at the Sun, 2001. (CSK Honor)

Stitches by Glen Huser. Groundwood, 2003.

The Way a Door Closes by Hope Anita Smith, illus. by Shane W. Evans. Henry Holt, 2003. (CSK–John Steptoe Winner)

Money Hungry

By Sharon G. Flake

N.Y., Hyperion/Jump at the Sun, 2001

Grade: 4–6

Genre: Fiction

Core Democratic Value: Equality

Everyone should get the same treatment, regardless of race, religion, economic status, or where one's parents or grandparents were born.

Content Perspective

Thirteen-year-old Raspberry Hill is starved for money and will do anything legal to get her hands on a dollar. She is obsessed, driven, and afraid of being homeless, so she keeps her eyes on the prize: the cold, hard cash. When the green stuff greases her palm, she gets comfort from feeling its crinkly paper power. Raspberry kisses her cash. She smells it. She loves it. But even money can't answer the questions that keep her awake at night. Will she and her Momma ever move out of the projects? How can she convince her friends to participate in her get-rich-quick schemes? Where is their next dollar coming from? Raspberry never wants to be homeless again.

Discussion Openers

Students should provide examples of text and/or illustrations to support their responses.

- Keeping in mind the core democratic value of equality, what were the life experiences that contributed to Raspberry's obsession with money?
- Mai's father is Chinese and her mother is black. Do you agree with the way Kevin treated Mai regarding her racial mix? Why or why not?
- What ideas justify Raspberry's mother throwing all of Raspberry's money out the window?

- Ja'nae owed Raspberry two hundred dollars. Do you agree with Raspberry's decision to take the fifty dollars from Ja'nae's table? Why or why not?
- Why did Zora's behavior toward Raspberry change when she discovered that her dad was dating Raspberry's mother?

Beyond the Book

- Write an alternative ending to *Money Hungry*.
- Which character in Raspberry's circle of friends is most like you? Explain.
- Would you like to have a friend like Raspberry? Why or why not?
- Using a thesaurus, find as many slang words and phrases for money as you can. Create a word search puzzle to share with your friends.
- Research homeless statistics in your community and share the information with classmates.

Books for Further Discussions

As Good As Anybody: Martin Luther King, Jr. and Abraham Joshua Heschel's Amazing March Toward Freedom by Richard Michelson, illus. by Raúl Colón. Knopf, 2008. (Sydney Taylor Award)

Chill Wind by Janet McDonald. Farrar, Straus and Giroux, 2002. (CSK–John Steptoe Winner)

One Crazy Summer by Rita Williams-Garcia. HarperCollins/Amistad, 2010. (CSK, Newbery)

Rosa by Nikki Giovanni, illus. by Bryan Collier. Henry Holt, 2005. (Caldecott, CSK)

Sit-In: How Four Friends Stood Up by Sitting Down by Andrea Davis Pinkney, illus. by Brian Pinkney. Little, Brown, 2010.

The Negro Speaks of Rivers

By Langston Hughes,
illus. by E. B. Lewis
N.Y., Hyperion/Jump at the Sun,
2009

Grade: 3–10

Genre: Poetry

Core Democratic Value: Liberty

Central to the idea of liberty is the understanding that the political or personal obligations of parents or ancestors cannot be legitimately forced on people.

Content Perspective

E. B. Lewis illustrates *The Negro Speaks of Rivers* with detailed elegance befitting one of Langston Hughes's best-known poems. Each double-spread page offers one line of the poem, and the illustrations fill in the details. Deep, rich colors saturate the pages, emphasizing the soul that "has grown deep like rivers," the rivers that hold secrets of a changing world.

Discussion Openers

Students should provide examples of text and/or illustrations to support their responses.

- In the first illustration, there is no sign of a river. What does the person in the picture know of rivers?
- The Nile, Euphrates, and Mississippi Rivers are all mentioned in this Langston Hughes poem. How are they related to the African American experience?
- What do E. B. Lewis's illustrations tell us about the relationship between people and rivers?
- How does E. B. Lewis use color to express mood?
- Look at the illustration about the Nile. Discuss the river's importance to the people standing in the river.

- Create a story about the mother and child in the illustration of the hut near the Congo.

Beyond the Book

- Explore the history of the Nile River at www.bbc.co.uk/history /ancient/egyptians/nile_01.shtml. Explain its importance to the people of ancient Egypt.
- Use online resources to explore the history of the Euphrates River. What would happen if the Euphrates dried up?
- Using online resources, research Abraham Lincoln's early political career. How did the Mississippi River help form his attitude about slavery?
- Explore the history of the Mississippi River. What role does the river play in American history?
- Rivers are important to preserving our natural environment. Identify a river close to where you live and volunteer to help keep it clean.

Books for Further Discussions

Going North by Janice N. Harrington, illus. by Jerome Lagarrigue. Melanie Kroupa, 2004.

The Great Migration: An American Story, illus. by Jacob Lawrence with a poem by Walter Dean Myers. HarperCollins, 1993. (Woodson Honor)

Moses: When Harriet Tubman Led Her People to Freedom by Carole Boston Weatherford, illus. by Kadir Nelson. Hyperion/Jump at the Sun, 2006. (CSK Winner, Caldecott Honor)

Twelve Rounds to Glory: The Story of Muhammad Ali by Charles R. Smith Jr., illus. by Bryan Collier. Candlewick, 2007. (CSK Honor)

We Are the Ship: The Story of Negro League Baseball by Kadir Nelson. Hyperion, 2008. (CSK Winner, Sibert Winner, Orbis Pictus Honor)

Ninth Ward

By Jewell Parker Rhodes
N.Y., Little, Brown, 2010
Grade: 4–6
Genre: Contemporary Realistic Fiction
Core Democratic Value: Life
Each person has the right to protect his or her life.

Content Perspective

Regional mystic elements are integrated into this realistic fiction portrayal of New Orleans during Hurricane Katrina. Lanesha and Mama Ya-Ya, Lanesha's adopted grandmother, are both gifted with the ability to see spirits ("sight"). Lanesha's story of survival extends beyond the storm; she successfully overcomes the limitation of caul over her eyes, the loss of her mother at childbirth, and the subsequent rejection by her mother's family. The various ways people coped with Katrina are explored, and the horrifying details are not spared.

Discussion Openers

Students should provide examples of text and/or illustrations to support their responses.

- Lanesha has a passion for words and a love of math. Describe how she uses math in everyday life and for survival.
- Describe the art on the cover. What do you think Lanesha is feeling?
- Make a list of your favorite words. Compare your list to Lanesha's list.
- Prepare a flowchart showing the sequence of events in the story.
- Pretend you are Lanesha and write a diary of what happens for the two days following being discovered and pulled to safety by the rescue boat.
- Retitle the book. Give a justification for your new title.

Beyond the Book

- Make a list of the ways you use math in everyday life.
- Investigate the meaning of *caul*. Write a short paragraph using the word.
- Research natural disasters in the United States. Make a list of examples of the ways disasters have affected people's lives. Consider instances of displacement, poverty, and recovery.
- Create a list of favorite words. Add to it throughout the term.
- What safety measures are in place in your community in the event of a weather emergency? Are they different for home and school?

Books for Further Discussions

Everything on a Waffle by Polly Horvath. Farrar, Straus and Giroux, 2001. (Newbery Honor)

Forged by Fire by Sharon M. Draper. Atheneum, 1997. (CSK Winner)

The Fourteenth Amendment: Equal Protection Under the Law by David L. Hudson, Jr. Enslow, 2002.

The People Could Fly: American Black Folktales

Told by Virginia Hamilton,
illus. by Leo and Diane Dillon
N.Y., Knopf, 1985
Genre: Folklore
Grade: 4–8
Core Democratic Value: Liberty
Liberty includes the freedom to believe what you want, to choose your own friends, to have your own ideas and opinions, to express your ideas in public, to meet in groups, and to have any lawful job or business.

Content Perspective

Tales of enslaved people from Africa are told in the voice of Virginia Hamilton. These folktales embody the lives of black people, providing a stage for their fanciful imaginations, their fear and coexistence with the supernatural, and their longings for freedom. The stories further reflect the life and culture of the South before the Civil War.

Discussion Openers

Students should provide examples of text and/or illustrations to support their responses.

- Read Virginia Hamilton's introduction. What was her purpose in collecting and writing these tales?
- Pick a favorite illustration. Explain how the illustration fits the accompanying tale.
- Identify the themes or central ideas of three titles in the chapter titled "Carrying the Run-aways."
- Assign one of the following character traits to each of the stories in the chapter titled "The Beautiful Girl of the Moon Tower": responsibility, honesty, caring, sharing, the golden rule, respect.

- Choose a chapter and make a chart of the survival strategies used by enslaved people.

Beyond the Book

- Prepare an introduction of Brer Fox that might be given to readers who are reading stories about his escapades for the first time.
- Read the Tales of the Supernatural in the chapter titled "John and the Devil's Daughter." Which tale or tales are geographically specific (i.e., could take place only in a warm climate)? Explain why.
- Compare Virginia Hamilton's Brer Fox to the same character in Julius Lester's *Tales of Uncle Remus.*
- Define the term *trickster tales;* locate examples from three additional collections.
- Research black folktales written in the Gullah dialect. Share three interesting observations with your classmates.

Books for Further Discussions

Elijah of Buxton by Christopher Paul Curtis. Scholastic, 2007. (CSK Winner, Newbery Honor, Jane Addams Honor, Scott O'Dell Winner)

Freedom Riders: John Lewis and Jim Zwerg on the Front Lines of the Civil Rights Movement by Ann Bausum, forewords by Freedom Riders Congressman John Lewis and Jim Zwerg. National Geographic, 2006. (Orbis Pictus, Sibert Honor)

Let It Shine: Stories of Black Women Freedom Fighters by Andrea Davis Pinkney, illus. by Stephen Alcorn. Harcourt, 2000. (Woodson Winner, CSK Honor)

Show Way by Jacqueline Woodson, illus. by Hudson Talbott. Putnam, 2005. (Newbery Honor)

Remember: The Journey to School Integration

By Toni Morrison
N.Y., Houghton Mifflin
Grade: 4–6
Genre: Nonfiction
Core Democratic Value: Justice
All people should be treated fairly in getting the advantages and disadvantages of our country.

Content Perspective

Through archival photographs Morrison shares the experiences of school integration. The roles that children and adults played bring the struggles for justice to the forefront. A civil rights and school integration timeline along with photographic reference notes and a dedication to the four children who died in the Birmingham church bombing are included at the end of the book.

Discussion Openers

Students should provide examples of text and/or illustrations to support their responses.

- The struggle to integrate schools in the South has been described as a time when "children had to be braver than their parents." What circumstances, events, or situations made this statement true?
- Reread the author's introduction and look at the photographs on pages 1 to 15. Describe the conditions that led to the Supreme Court decision of 1964.
- Look at the picture on page 13 and read the photo reference on page 74. Discuss ways in which toys influence children's perception of place in society.

- Select a photograph of your choice and describe what you see in that photograph. Discuss what the person or persons might be thinking.
- The book is illustrated with black-and-white photographs. Why did the author, photographer, or publisher choose that medium?

Beyond the Book

- Compare your school experience with those of the children in the book.
- Research the *Brown v. Board of Education* case online. www.nps.gov /brvb/index.htm. Write a brief description of the case.
- Identify the people in the photographs on pages 44, 63, 64, and 72. Discuss the contributions each made to the civil rights movement.
- Think about how the civil rights movement spread to restaurants, theaters, and other public facilities. Discuss with your class why you believe this happened.
- Make a case for children's right to fair and equal treatment.

Books for Further Discussions

The Lions of Little Rock by Kristin Levine. Putnam, 2012.

Mississippi Challenge by Mildred Pitts Walter. Bradbury, 1992. (CSK Honor, Woodson Winner)

The Road to Memphis by Mildred D. Taylor. Dial, 1990. (CSK Winner)

The Story of Ruby Bridges by Robert Coles, illus. by George Ford. Scholastic, 1995.

The Road to Paris

By Nikki Grimes
N.Y., Putnam, 2006
Grade: 4–6
Genre: Fiction
Core Democratic Value:
Pursuit of Happiness
People have the right to pursue happiness in their own way, as long as they do not infringe on the rights of others.

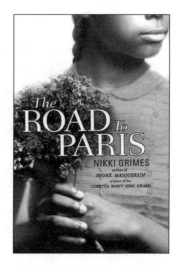

Content Perspective

Paris Richmond is a resilient biracial eight-year-old, neglected by an alcoholic mother and shifted from foster home to foster home. When her brother, two years older and labeled incorrigible, goes to a group home, the separation becomes almost unbearable. Through the intervention of a loving foster mother, Paris gets a glimpse of life in a happy family, although she longs for reunion with her brother. When her birth mother decides to reclaim her children, Paris must choose between the stable life she enjoys in her foster home or a return to her unreliable mother with a promise that her brother would join them. With strong characterization and spare prose, Grimes offers the reader a memorable protagonist whose strength comes from keeping "God in her pocket."

Discussion Openers

Students should provide examples of text and/or illustrations to support their responses.

- The author tags Paris as "frightened girl." What was she afraid of?
- Malcolm stole money from his foster mother, Mrs. Boone, just before he and Paris ran away. Is stealing always wrong?
- Describe Malcolm. Would you like to have a brother like him? Why or why not?
- What does this story tell us about justice, equality, and the pursuit of happiness? How are they related?

- The Lincolns were Paris's foster parents, and Miss Liberty was her case worker. What is the significance of these names?

Beyond the Book

- Paris tells David a secret and he promises not to reveal it to anyone. When is it okay to divulge a secret?
- After reading *The Road to Paris,* read Jacqueline Woodson's *Locomotion* and discuss how foster care is presented in each.
- Create a bullying scenario and dramatize positive interventions.
- List responsibilities that come with the right to pursue happiness.
- Make a list of things that might make you happy. What effect would achieving those things have on other people?

Books for Further Discussions

Brendan Buckley's Universe and Everything in It by Sundee T. Frazier. Delacorte, 2007. (CSK–John Steptoe Winner)

Bud, Not Buddy by Christopher Paul Curtis. Delacorte, 1999. (CSK Winner, Newbery Winner)

Harlem Summer by Walter Dean Myers. Scholastic, 2007.

Money Hungry by Sharon G. Flake. 2001. Hyperion/Jump at the Sun, (CSK Honor)

Stitches by Glen Huser. Groundwood, 2003.

Standing Against the Wind

By Traci L. Jones
N.Y., Farrar, Straus and Giroux, 2006
Grade: 4–6
Genre: Contemporary Realistic Fiction
Core Democratic Value:
Pursuit of Happiness
All people can find happiness in their own way, as long as they do not step on the rights of others.

Content Perspective

Snatched away from her comfortable home in Georgia and forced to live with her aunt in Chicago while her mother serves time in jail, thirteen-year-old Patrice faces a daunting year. Her sense of alienation is palpable as she is ridiculed for her "puffy" hair and bullied by streetwise boys. Encouraged by her school principal and her savvy friend, Monty, shy Patrice begins to imagine a way out. With confidence and determination she applies for a scholarship to an African American boarding school but faces one last hurdle, her jailed mother's signed permission. Can she overcome this last stumbling block and access her mother before the deadline? Traci L. Jones brings Patrice's dilemma to life with understanding and compassion.

Discussion Openers

Students should provide examples of text and/or illustrations to support their responses.

- Patrice has several obstacles to overcome. How do they challenge her pursuit of happiness?
- What character traits does Patrice exhibit that help her overcome the obstacles?
- How are Patrice and her sister, Cherise, similar? How are they different?

- How does Patrice change over the course of the story?
- Peer pressure can make you behave or say something you wouldn't otherwise. Discuss the role of peer pressure in the story.

Beyond the Book

- Who was Mary McLeod Bethune? Why did Patrice choose her as a topic for her historical essay?
- Listen to the portrayal of Mary McLeod Bethune at www.lkwdpl .org/wihohio/beth-mar.htm and discuss similarities between Mary McLeod Bethune's early life and that of Patrice.
- Start a journal in which you write about your thoughts and feelings concerning school. Which parts of your journal would you share with teachers, friends, and classmates, and which parts would you share with family or not at all?
- Have you ever been bullied? How did it make you feel?
- Have you ever bullied someone else? How did that make you feel?

Books for Further Discussions

Bud, Not Buddy by Christopher Paul Curtis. Scholastic, 1999. (CSK Winner, Newbery Winner)

Celeste's Harlem Renaissance by Eleanora E. Tate. Little, Brown, 2007.

Lizzie Bright and The Buckminster Boy by Gary D. Schmidt. Clarion, 2004. (Newbery Honor, Printz Honor)

Money Hungry by Sharon G. Flake. Hyperion/Jump at the Sun, 2001. (CSK Honor)

The Way a Door Closes by Hope Anita Smith, illus. by Shane W. Evans. Henry Holt, 2003. (CSK–John Steptoe Winner)

Talkin' About Bessie: The Story of Aviator Elizabeth Coleman

By Nikki Grimes, illus. by E. B. Lewis
N.Y., Orchard, 2002

Grade: 4–6

Genre: Biography

Core Democratic Value: Justice

All people should be treated fairly in getting the advantages and disadvantages of our country. No group or person should be favored.

Content Perspective

Nikki Grimes's poetic vignettes speak to the realities of Bessie Coleman's life: her birth in a dirt-floor cabin and her hard work in field, laundry, beauty shop, and school. Triumphs as an aviator were tragically interrupted by her demise at the age of thirty-four. E. B. Lewis's attention to historic detail highlights Bessie's determination, excitement, pride, and joy. Grimes inspires and challenges her readers to be like Bessie. Together Grimes and Lewis have created a book that soars.

Discussion Openers

Students should provide examples of text and/or illustrations to support their responses.

- Discuss the major impediments to Bessie's desire to amount to something some day.
- Bessie took pleasure in the most difficult and tedious aspects of flight school training. Discuss the possible reasons for her passion.
- What does the laundry customer's assessment of Bessie's demeanor say about how she views herself and her future?
- Why did Bessie embellish her accomplishments when speaking to youth groups and the press?

- What evidence does author Grimes provide that Bessie was a positive person?
- Who were the people in Bessie's life who believed in her determination to learn to fly?

Beyond the Book

- Research aviator gear worn by pilots in the 1920s.
- Elizabeth Coleman earned her pilot license in France. Research the institution that awarded her a license.
- Research the practice of barnstorming. Discuss the balance of pilot safety and audience entertainment.
- Research women pilots in the 1920s and 1930s. Who were they?
- What role did the Negro press play in the life and career of Coleman?

Books for Further Discussions

Claudette Colvin: Twice Toward Justice by Phillip Hoose. Farrar/Kroupa, 2009. (Newbery Honor, Sibert Honor, Woodson Winner, Jane Addams Honor)

Let It Shine: Stories of Black Women Freedom Fighters by Andrea Davis Pinkney. Harcourt, 2000. (CSK Honor, Woodson Winner)

Sonia Sotomayor: First Hispanic U.S. Supreme Court Justice by Lisa Tucker. Lerner, 2010.

The Watsons Go to Birmingham— 1963: A Novel

By Christopher Paul Curtis
N.Y., Delacorte, 1995
Grade: 5–8
Genre: Fiction
Core Democratic Value: Equality
Everyone should get the same treatment, regardless of race, religion, economic status, or where one's parents or grandparents were born.

Content Perspective

Christopher Paul Curtis skillfully interweaves the comic, tragic, and emotionally engaging lives of the Watson family as they travel to Birmingham, Alabama, at the height of the civil rights struggle. A comic family story of hilarious dimensions to be sure, but also one that will allow readers a close encounter with the realities of the segregated South.

Discussion Openers

Students should provide examples of text and/or illustrations to support their responses.

- What was the feeling of the Watson boys about welfare? Why did they feel that way?
- What do you suppose would have happened if Byron had made his so-called prison break before the planned trip to Birmingham?
- Byron, Kenny, and Joey each responded differently to the trip to Birmingham. Describe and discuss their perceptions.
- Kenny says, "The worse trouble you get into the more steps it takes." Do you agree with Kenny that getting into trouble generally happens in steps? Why or why not?
- What evidence in the story suggests the Watson boys engaged in competitive sibling interactions?

Beyond the Book

- Construct a character trait chart of three of your siblings or friends. Compare it to that of the Watson family.
- Define the term *hero*. Locate a news story about a hero and compare it to your definition.
- Research the role of children in the civil rights movement. How did adults react to young people entering the struggle?
- Locate newspaper accounts of the Birmingham bombing event. Share details missing from the Watson family's experience with your classmates.
- Writers often use comedy to lighten the effects of tragic events. Brainstorm ways that comedians use this technique.

Books for Further Discussions

I Have a Sister, My Sister Is Deaf by Jeanne Whitehouse Peterson. HarperCollins, 1977. (CSK Honor)

Mississippi Challenge by Mildred Pitts Walter. Bradbury, 1992. (CSK Honor)

The Road to Memphis by Mildred Taylor. Dial, 1990. (CSK Winner)

The Way a Door Closes

By Hope Anita Smith,
illus. by Shane W. Evans
N.Y., Henry Holt, 2003

Grade: 4–6

Genre: Contemporary Realistic Fiction/Poetry

Core Democratic Value:

Pursuit of Happiness

All people can find happiness in their own way, as long as they do not step on the rights of others.

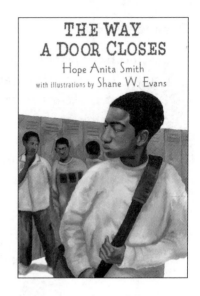

Content Perspective

Thirty-four gentle poems slowly reveal the details of thirteen-year-old C.J.'s life. At first his contemporary family is "just like the sun / and we are all / golden." But when his father leaves abruptly, everything changes, and Smith's poems show C.J.'s anger and confusion. The eventual ending is a hopeful blessing.

Discussion Openers

Students should provide examples of text and/or illustrations to support their responses.

- *The Way a Door Closes* tells us a lot about the people in C.J.'s life. The poem "Telling Tales" tells a different story. What does that poem tell us about C.J.'s living conditions?
- What did Grandmomma mean when she said, "There are a lot of ways of leaving. / Your daddy / left / a while ago. / Now, he's just gone"?
- How does C.J. feel about his family? How can you tell?
- What does *The Way a Door Closes* tell us about the pursuit of happiness?

- What happens to happiness when a father walks out the door? What did Momma mean when she said, "You just changed the course of history"?
- How are the first poem, "Golden," and the last poem, "Astronomy 101," alike?

Beyond the Book

- Reread the poem "History Lesson" and then research the topic of Jim Crow laws. Discuss how these laws may have affected family life.
- Doors are an important part of *The Way a Door Closes*. Write a poem about what you notice about the doors in your life.
- Reread the poem "Telling Tales" and write a poem about your wildest dreams. Discuss how you might achieve your dreams.
- Identify a positive male role model in your life. What makes him so?
- People say when one door closes, another one opens. What does this mean?

Books for Further Discussions

The Journey Home by Isabelle Holland. Scholastic, 1990.

Keeping the Night Watch by Hope Anita Smith, illus. by E. B. Lewis. Henry Holt, 2009.

Locomotion by Jacqueline Woodson. Putnam, 2003. (CSK Honor)

The Red Rose Box by Brenda Woods. Putnam, 2002. (CSK Honor)

Which Way Freedom?

By Joyce Hansen

N.Y., Walker, 1986

Grade: 5–9

Genre: Historical Fiction

Core Democratic Value: Equality

Everyone should get the same treatment, regardless of race, religion, economic status, or where one's parents or grandparents were born. All people have political, social, and economic equality.

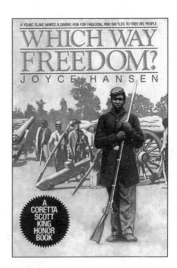

Content Perspective

Author Joyce Hansen's historical novel for young readers focuses on the seldom-illuminated role of enslaved people fighting in the Civil War. Some 200,000 blacks fought in the Civil War, and Obi, the hero of Hansen's story, was one of them. He is pictured as one who never acclimated to the subservient role of slave, forever looking for the chance to run and find his mother, Lorena. The fact that scores of black people managed to gather information about safe routes, Yankee soldier activities, and the various masters under which so-called freedom could be found is no less than miraculous in itself.

Discussion Openers

Students should provide examples of text and/or illustrations to support their responses.

- Provide evidence from the text to support Daniel's statement: "Slave don't have nothin' belong to he—not he woman, child, cabin—not even heself."
- Discuss the impact of the fact that Obi had only one name. How was it resolved? What meaning might that resolution have today?
- Buka stopped Obi from running in one of his early attempts. What did Buka mean when he said, "You gotta know where freedom start"?

- Why did Easter insist that Jason not be left behind when the opportunity to escape presented itself? Was this a good idea? Why or why not?
- Discuss Obi's adjustment to military life. Include his name, uniform, skills, friendships, and pay.

Beyond the Book

- If you were to make a movie of *Which Way Freedom?*, which five scenes would you pick for high drama?
- Provide evidence that enlistment in the Union Army did not end discriminatory treatment for formerly enslaved men.
- Research online for information about the handmade boats often used by indigenous cultures similar to the one Obi used to escape. Share your findings with your classmates.
- What does it say about the effectiveness of security on plantations given the fact that some 200,000 African Americans managed to escape slavery to fight in the Civil War? Discuss the strategies used to prevent and recapture runaways.
- What evidence is there that blacks in the northern states suffered a different kind of prejudice before and during the Civil War?

Books for Further Discussions

At Her Majesty's Request: An African Princess in Victorian England by Walter Dean Myers. Scholastic, 1999. (Orbis Pictus Winner)

The Rock and the River by Kekla Magoon. Aladdin, 2009. (CSK–John Steptoe Winner)

Twelve Rounds to Glory: The Story of Muhammad Ali by Charles R. Smith, Jr., illus by Bryan Collier. Candlewick, 2007. (CSK Honor)

We Are the Ship: The Story of Negro League Baseball by Kadir Nelson. Hyperion/Jump at the Sun, 2008. (CSK Winner/Honor, Orbis Pictus Honor, Sibert Winner)

Zora and Me

By Victoria Bond and T. R. Simon
N.Y., Candlewick, 2010
Grade: 4–8
Genre: Historical Fiction
Core Democratic Value: Liberty
Liberty includes the freedom to believe what
you want, to choose your own friends, to have
your own ideas and opinions, to express your
ideas in public, to meet in groups, and to have
any lawful job or business.

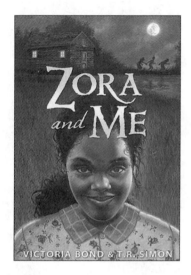

Content Perspective

Zora, Carrie, and Terry are best friends in the African American community of Eatonville, Florida, during the early 1900s. Carrie, the narrator
of the story, is the fictionalized young Zora Neale Hurston's best friend.
The unfairness of the Jim Crow South appears in stark contrast to the
caring community of Eatonville. The real appeal of this piece of historical fiction is the glimpse it provides into the childhood of Zora Neale
Hurston. It is a story of friendship, family, and community with a fine
balance between mystery and history.

Discussion Openers

Students should provide examples of text and/or illustrations to support
their responses.

- Carrie distinguishes between a "daddy's girl" and a "mama's girl."
  Which one best describes Zora's relationship to her parents? Explain.
- How did Mr. Hurston feel about white folks? Could he speak openly
  about his feelings?
- In addition to her mother, there are two men in Zora's life whom she
  trusts completely. Explain her relationship with them.
- The people of Eatonville could speak freely to each other while in the
  community. Why did their behavior have to change when they were
  outside the community?

- What made it more difficult for light-skinned African Americans to function in both the black community and in the white community?
- What was the lie referred to in the last line of chapter 12? Why did it have serious repercussions in the Eatonville community?

Beyond the Book

- Research the life of Zora Neale Hurston online and identify three facts about her life not covered in *Zora and Me*.
- Identify people in your life that you trust completely. Explain why they are trustworthy.
- Freedom of speech is an important freedom in a democratic society. Explain what it means to you and why it is important.
- The freedom to meet in groups is an essential component of a free democratic society. What would be the consequences if this freedom were denied?
- With every freedom comes responsibility. What might be a responsibility related to the freedom of speech and the freedom to meet in groups?

Books for Further Discussions

Bud, Not Buddy by Christopher Paul Curtis. Delacorte, 1999. (CSK Winner, Newbery Winner)

Elijah of Buxton by Christopher Paul Curtis. Scholastic, 2007. (CSK Winner, Newbery Honor, Jane Addams Honor)

The Road to Paris by Nikki Grimes. Putnam, 2006. (CSK Honor)

Standing Against the Wind by Traci L. Jones. Farrar, Straus and Giroux, 2006. (CSK–John Steptoe Winner)

CHAPTER 5

Grades 6–10

Becoming Billie Holiday

By Carole Boston Weatherford,
illus. by Floyd Cooper
N.Y., Wordsong, 2008
Grade: 7–9
Genre: Poetry
Core Democratic Value: Liberty/
Personal Freedom
*Every individual is free to act, think
and to believe.*

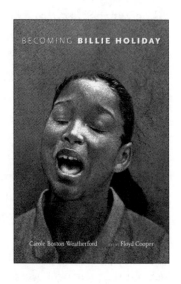

Content Perspective

Author Carole Boston Weatherford tells the story of legendary singer, Billie Holiday, born Eleanor Fagan. The voice of Billie comes through in this fictionalized account of pain, struggle, crime, and a deep longing for the security of her father's love. Weatherford's free verse poems bear the titles of Billie's iconic repertoire, speaking with honesty and poignancy of her passionate pursuit to become a singer.

Discussion Openers

Students should provide examples of text and/or illustrations to support their responses.

- In what ways did religion impact Billie's life and singing? Identify two poems that reveal something about Billie's beliefs.
- Billie lived in three cities—Philadelphia, Baltimore, and New York. How was her life similar in each city? How was it different?
- Billie's songs can be described as windows to her thoughts and feelings. Find three song titles that suggest sadness, three that say something about her childhood, and three that say something about the music in her life.
- Look at the first three illustrations in the book. What do the pictures tell you about Billie's early life?
- In what New York nightclubs did Billie Holiday perform? Which are still in existence? Identify other entertainers who performed at the same venues.

Beyond the Book

- Select one of Weatherford's verses and illustrate it using your own ideas, artistic medium, and technique.
- Plan and perform a spoken word/open mic program using poems from the book.
- Choose one of Billie Holiday's contemporaries from the list of biographies in the back. Research their life and share your findings with your classmates.
- Design a CD cover for a collection of songs by Billie.
- Using online resources look up the song "Strange Fruit." Share with your classmates any information you find about that song.

Books for Further Discussions

Bird by Shadra Strickland. Lee & Low, 2008. (CSK–John Steptoe Winner)

Flygirl by Sherri L. Smith. Putnam, 2008.

Twelve Rounds to Glory: The Story of Muhammad Ali by Charles R. Smith. Candlewick, 2007 (CSK Honor)

The Captive

By Joyce Hansen
N.Y., Scholastic, 1994
Grade: 5–8
Genre: Historical Fiction
Core Democratic Value: Justice
All people should be treated fairly in getting the advantages and disadvantages of our country. No group or person should be favored.

Content Perspective

Author Joyce Hansen breathes life into the character of Kofi, son of an Ashanti king. Kofi's life is turned upside down when the long-awaited tribal celebration turns into a horrific scene of murder, capture, and slavery. Kofi eventually finds himself sold to a New England master, where he and two others from the same ship experience the dichotomy of those who profess the sanctimony of faith yet would hold others in servitude. Kofi relishes the stolen opportunities to learn to read from his master's own wife. In time, Kofi finds a means of escape and falls into the protective hands of the famous African seaman Paul Cuffe. With Cuffe's help, Kofi travels back to Africa as a freedman.

Discussion Openers

Students should provide examples of text and/or illustrations to support their responses.

- Why did Kofi risk life and limb for the sake of a flute?
- What would have happened if Kofi, Joseph, and Tim had not been bought by the same master?
- Why did Kofi pretend ignorance at first when directed to complete simple house tasks?
- Do you agree with Master Browne's practice of praying over Kofi after a beating?
- Discuss the journey of Kofi's flute from Africa to New England and its importance throughout Kofi's enslavement in America.

- What did Kofi learn from his encounters with Oppong and Sharif?
- Describe Kofi's first reaction to the seasons in New England. Why did he find the seasons startling?

Beyond the Book

- What possible reasons did slaveholders have to believe enslaved Africans were naturally dull, backward, and incapable of learning anything beyond physically hard labor?
- Research Captain Paul Cuffe. Share three facts about his life that are recounted in *The Captive*.
- Research slavery in New England. What role did religion plan in how enslaved people were treated there?
- Research the Ashanti people and their role in the slave trade.
- The Ashanti are closely identified with the slave trade. Who are the Ashanti today?

Books for Further Discussions

I Thought My Soul Would Rise and Fly: The Diary of Patsy, a Freed Girl by Joyce Hansen. Scholastic, 1997. (CSK Honor)

The Land by Mildred Taylor. Penguin Putnam/Fogelman, 2001. (CSK Winner)

Which Way Freedom? by Joyce Hansen. Walker, 1986. (CSK Honor)

Carver:
A Life in Poems

By Marilyn Nelson
Ashville, N.C., Front Street, 2001
Grade: 6–9
Genre: Poetry/Biography
Core Democratic Value:
Pursuit of Happiness
People have the right to pursue happiness in
their own way, as long as they do not infringe
on the rights of others.

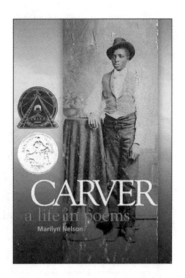

Content Perspective

The character and genius of Dr. George Washington Carver quietly unfolds through the artistic creation of poetry and scholarly investigation of letters and journal entries of the era. Dr. Carver's life story reflects a passion for learning and an unwillingness to accept defeat. Undaunted by the challenges of life and in spite of disappointments, he was always able to move forward. It is in his work that his spirit lives on.

Discussion Openers

Students should provide examples of text or illustrations to support their responses.

- Why did Carver repeatedly choose to do menial tasks to support himself as he pursued his education?
- Do you agree with Carver's view of people as expressed in "The New Rooster"?
- What, if anything, is significant about Carver's always wearing a flower in his lapel?
- What was the relationship between Carver and Booker T. Washington as revealed in Nelson's poetry? Find three poems that provide specific insights.

- Discuss Carver's mantra: "Nothing is wasted or permanently lost in nature."
- Describe three specific ways Dr. Carver shared his research and knowledge with others.
- Given what you have read about Carver and his ways of work, would you like to have worked for him? Why or why not?

Beyond the Book

- Select an event or incident described by Nelson in her biographical poetry about Carver. Using online resources, look for information left out or a point of view not mentioned in the event or incident you have selected.
- Research Carver's investigations into the abundant uses of wild plants. Can you find evidence that any of his discoveries have come into common use today?
- Carver was a private man. Research how he handled being in the national spotlight for his accomplishments.
- Research Booker T. Washington and his relationship with Carver. How did their views on race differ? How were they the same?
- Investigate Carver's educational experiences in Iowa. What impact did those experiences have on his career as an inventor?

Books for Further Discussions

The Legend of Buddy Bush by Shelia P. Moses. Simon & Schuster, 2004. (CSK Honor)

Life, After by Sarah Darer Littman. Scholastic, 2010. (Sydney Taylor Honor)

Stuck on Earth by David Klass. Farrar, Straus and Giroux, 2010.

Day of Tears

By Julius Lester
N.Y., Hyperion/Jump at the Sun, 2005
Genre: Historical Fiction
Grade: 6–9
Core Democratic Value: Liberty
*The right to liberty is considered an unalter-
able aspect of the human condition.*

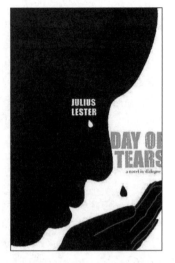

Content Perspective

Day of Tears is a masterful fictionalized
account of the largest slave auction in U.S.
history, held in Savannah, Georgia, 1859. In a powerfully dramatic format, the voices of enslaved African characters and their masters move
between monologues, interactive conversations, and reflective memories years later. This novel allows the reader to understand the moral
dilemmas faced by slaveholders and the powerlessness of the slaves.
Julius Lester validates the challenges of both to affirm humanity in the
midst of slavery.

Discussion Openers

Students should provide examples of text and/or illustrations that
support their response.

- Author Julius Lester uses internal and external conversations along
  with flashback as a writing technique. What are the advantages and
  disadvantages of this writing style?
- What consequences in the story can you identify as outcomes of the
  largest slave auction in history?
- Extract all of the justifications for the institution of slavery you can
  find in the text. Do any of these justifications benefit the enslaved
  person?
- Identify white people in the story who showed compassion for the
  slaves. Discuss the positive and negative aspects of the relationship
  between the enslaved and empathetic white people.

• Discuss the possible outcomes of an enslaved person's decision to run away. What did this say about the institution of slavery?

Beyond the Book

• Research the lyrics to the freedom song, "Follow the Drinking Gourd." What was its purpose?
• Research which states were Confederate and which were not. Discuss reasons why.
• Visit the National Underground Railroad Freedom Center website (www.freedomcenter.org). Explore routes used by escaping slaves.
• Explore the differences between indentured servants and slavery.
• Research and find notes on the Underground Railroad that led to freedom in Canada.

Books for Further Discussions

Before We Were Free by Julia Alvarez. Knopf, 2002. (Pura Belpre Winner)

Days of Jubilee: The End of Slavery in the United States by Patricia C. and Fredrick L. McKissack. Scholastic, 2003. (CSK Honor)

Elijah of Buxton by Christopher Paul Curtis. Scholastic, 2007. (CSK Winner, Jane Addams Honor)

Escape to Freedom: A Play About Young Frederick Douglass by Ossie Davis. S. French, 1977. (CSK Winner, Jane Addams Honor)

Junius Over Far

By Virginia Hamilton
N.Y., Harper & Row, 1985
Grade: 6–9
Genre: Realistic Fiction
Core Democratic Value:
Pursuit of Happiness
It is the right of citizens in the United States to pursue happiness in their own way, as long as they do not infringe upon the rights of others.

Content Perspective

Junius's relationship with aged Grandfather Jackabo is more special than his Americanized father would prefer. Junius regularly chooses Grandfather Jackabo's island lessons and stories of the Greater Antilles instead of hanging out with classmates at Mary and Slims for malts or hot chocolate. The elderly Jackabo is "wastin away from homesickness" for Snake Island, the Caribbean isle of his youth. When Jakabo returns to Snake, he finds both his former dilapidated dwelling at the Rawlings Estate and Burtie Rawlings, son of the family that he worked for. Though the two never liked each other, they manage to forge a peaceful living arrangement. All is not peaceful, however, when Burtie disappears after sticking his nose into the doings of his absentee island neighbors. It is Junius and his persistent badgering of his dad to travel to Snake that brings the three generations safely together in harmony.

Discussion Openers

Students should provide examples of text and/or illustrations to support their responses.

- Make an outline of ways the story might be different if told by Burt Rawlings.
- Select three chapters from the book. Write a subtitle for each that reflects the events covered.

- What people, places, or events in the story would you like to know more about?
- Identify those elements of the story that speak directly to Junius's character.
- Design a paperback cover for the story that is different from the original.

Beyond the Book

- Search online for information about Snake Island. Use your findings to prepare a travel advertisement.
- Research what types of criminal activities are most often committed in the islands by foreigners.
- Which elements of high school might be most difficult to adjust to for a student moving from a Caribbean island to the United States?
- What are the positives and negatives of intergenerational relationships?

Books for Further Discussions

Bird by Zetta Elliott, illus. by Shadra Strickland. Lee & Low, 2008. (CSK–John Steptoe Winner)

Blue Jasmine by Kashmira Sheth. Hyperion, 2004.

The Red Rose Box by Brenda Woods. Putnam, 2002. (CSK Honor)

Songs of Faith by Angela Johnson. Orchard, 1998.

Toning the Sweep by Angela Johnson. Orchard, 1993. (CSK Winner)

The Legend of Buddy Bush

By Shelia P. Moses
N.Y., McElderry, 2004
Grade: 6–12
Genre: Historical Fiction
Core Democratic Value: Liberty
The right to liberty is considered an unalterable aspect of the human condition. It includes personal freedom, political freedom, and economic freedom.

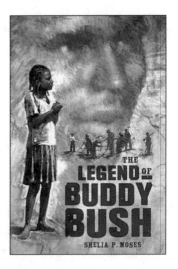

Content Perspective

This compelling story told by twelve-year-old Pattie Mae Shoals is a blend of truth and fiction. Buddy Bush was actually a real person. Pattie's dreams for a better life in New York City come firsthand from her Uncle Buddy, who has returned from the big city without explanation, (at least to Pattie) to live and work in Rich Square, North Carolina, with a new way of thinking. Buddy's life in the big city has made him less tolerant of the restrictions on people of color in 1947. His effort to live and work in Rich Square without bending to the senseless constraints of southern prejudices eventually leads him to an encounter with the Ku Klux Klan.

Discussion Openers

Students should provide examples of text and/or illustrations to support their responses.

- How did Buddy Bush become a legend?
- Author Shelia Moses captures much of the wisdom of the South in the characters' picturesque language. What meaning might you see today in Grandpa's statement: "Don't let nothin that you can change worry you" or Uncle Buddy's statement: ". . . the young are strong, but the old know the way"?

- Buddy was arrested because a white woman claimed he made a pass at her. Why would she make this accusation?
- The black community was confident that Buddy Bush had done nothing wrong. How did the people show their support?
- Discuss the new way of thinking that Buddy Bush brought back from New York City.

Beyond the Book

- Uncle Buddy was asked whether he would be chopping cotton. He replied that the only cotton he would be picking would be his T-shirt off the floor. Research the journey of cotton from seed to shirt.
- Locate the town of Rich Square on a map of North Carolina. What additional information can you find about Rich Square today?
- On page 147, Pattie Mae writes to her sister, BarJean, that Grandma and Grandpa have a telephone and it is yellow. When did telephone companies begin making nonblack phones?
- Discuss the use of group singing and spiritual songs in the 1960s struggle for equal rights.
- What was the Ku Klux Klan? In which states was the Klan most active?

Books for Further Discussions

Francie by Karen English. Farrar, Straus and Giroux, 1999. (CSK Honor)

The Road to Memphis by Mildred D. Taylor. Dial, 1990. (CSK Winner)

Roll of Thunder, Hear My Cry by Mildred D. Taylor. Dial, 1976. (Newbery Winner, CSK Honor, Jane Addams Honor)

Sweet Whispers, Brother Rush by Virginia Hamilton. Philomel, 1982. (CSK Winner, Newbery Honor)

A Long Hard Journey: The Story of the Pullman Porter

Patricia and Fredrick McKissack

By Patricia and Fredrick McKissack

N.Y., Walker, 1989

Grade: 5–9

Genre: Nonfiction

Core Democratic Value: Justice

People should be treated fairly in the distribution of the benefits and burdens of society, the correction of wrongs and injuries, the gathering of information, and the making of decisions.

Content Perspective

The role of the black porter is integral to the development of railroads as a mode of inter- and intrastate transportation in the United States. Dining and sleeping cars evolved from primitive accommodations to well-appointed moving hospitality suites. The successful growth of these travel services is due to the vision of one George Pullman and the availability of a large labor force in the form of recently freed slave laborers. The abuse of these travel porters, originally grateful for steady employment, led to an unlikely first: the development of a labor union initiated and controlled by Negroes. The Brotherhood of Sleeping Car Porters, under the persistent and capable leadership of Asa Philip Randolph, survived a battle that is often portrayed as a David and Goliath struggle because of the unequal strength of the two sides. The porters endured personal threats, frequent firings, and almost nonexistent funds.

Discussion Openers

Students should provide examples of text and/or illustrations to support their responses.

• Describe the constraints endured by early Pullman porters as they went about their duties.

- How and why did management attempt to control the porters' access to information? In what ways were they successful or unsuccessful?
- Who were the sleeping car conductors? What was their role in the Pullman porters' attempt to organize?
- Identify and discuss the roles of three leaders in the struggle to organize a porters' union.
- Describe George Pullman as an innovator.

Beyond the Book

- Discuss how the following influenced the organization of the Pullman porter union: The Messenger, Booker T. Washington, Ladies Auxiliary.
- How did the U.S. Railroad Administration and the Transportation Act of 1920 impact the lives of Pullman porters?
- Make a timeline showing the ongoing initiatives instituted by the Pullman Company to squelch organizing activities.
- Identify three legendary heroes of the railroads.
- Discuss the porters' descriptions of tipping and tippers.

Books for Further Discussions

Birmingham Sunday by Larry Dane Brimner. Calkins Creek, 2010. (Jane Addams Honor, Orbis Pictus Honor)

Bucking the Sarge by Christopher Paul Curtis. Wendy Lamb, 2004.

Sweet Thang by Allison Whittenberg. Delacorte, 2006.

A Thousand Never Evers by Shana Burg. Delacorte, 2008.

The Watsons Go to Birmingham—1963 by Christopher Paul Curtis. Delacorte, 1995. (Newbery Honor, Jane Addams Honor, CSK Honor)

Mare's War

By Tanita S. Davis
N.Y., Knopf, 2009
Grade: 6–10
Genre: Fiction
Core Democratic Value: Equality
*Everyone should get the same treatment,
regardless of race, religion, economic status,
or where one's parents or grandparents were
born. All people have political, social, and
economic equality.*

Content Perspective

A road trip with Mare, a spirited and opinionated grandmother, and her two thoroughly modern granddaughters makes for one memorable time. There is a lot more to Mare than Octavia and Tali know. As the miles slowly unfold, Mare's story of her harrowing younger days with the Women's Army Corps in World War II comes to life. Though the girls start out as unwilling passengers, their view of the world changes as they fall under the spell of their grandmother's storytelling. Rich details of the lives of African American servicewomen add a historical perspective and appreciation of their grandmother and the times in which she lived.

Discussion Openers

Students should provide examples of text and/or illustrations to support their responses.

- How did the sisters' attitudes and demeanors change as the story unfolded? Make a list of adjectives that reveal those changes at the beginning and the end of the story.
- What message about equality was Mare trying to give her granddaughters? Was she successful?
- Organize the book into three sections. How would you label each section?

- Find a passage in the story that best describes the kind of person Mare was.
- How would you like to have Mare for your grandmother? Why or why not?

Beyond the Book

- Create an online map of the trip from Los Angeles to Louisiana. Place markers at each stop.
- Research the jobs that women were allowed to do in the Women's Army Corps in Mare's time. Compare those jobs to the jobs they are allowed to do today.
- Military uniforms have changed over the years. Find photographs of the WAC uniforms in World War II and compare them to current army uniforms.
- Did the book give you any new ideas about yourself? Your grandmother or older relatives?
- Contact your local Women's Army Corp organization to arrange an interview with WACs from World War II.

Books for Further Discussions

Elijah of Buxton by Christopher Paul Curtis. Scholastic, 2007. (CSK Winner, Newbery Winner, Scott O'Dell Winner, Jane Addams Honor)

The Lions of Little Rock by Kristin Levine. Putnam, 2012.

The Rock and the River by Kekla Magoon. Aladdin, 2009. (CSK–John Steptoe Winner)

Somewhere in the Darkness by Walter Dean Myers. Scholastic, 1992. (CSK Honor, Newberry Honor)

Martin Luther King, Jr. and the Freedom Movement

By Lillie Patterson

N.Y., Facts on File, 1989

Grade: 6–8

Genre: Historical Fiction

Core Democratic Value: Liberty

The right to liberty includes personal freedom, political freedom, and economic freedom.

Content Perspective

Lillie Patterson captures the essence of Martin Luther King, Jr. as freedom fighter in *Martin Luther King, Jr. and the Freedom Movement*. It chronicles King's life from his early years as a Baptist minister to the march on Washington, to serving jail time for participating in peaceful demonstrations. Every aspect of Patterson's story resounds with a mighty cry for freedom and equality. She focuses on King's global perspective of freedom for all people and describes his nonviolent means of achieving it. She does not neglect the controversies that sometimes played out in King's life and tells his story from a very personal, human perspective. Patterson's book provides a thorough introduction to the civil rights movement and is a strong indicator of just how far we still have to go to achieve freedom and equality for all. Included is a timeline of significant civil rights events, as well as music and lyrics to many freedom songs of the era.

Discussion Openers

Students should provide examples of text and/or illustrations to support their responses.

- Governor Faubus declared that Central High was off limits to blacks. He said that "blood would run in the streets" if black students attempted to enter the school. How does Faubus's thinking contradict King's perspective?
- Why did the school superintendent ask the parents of the Little Rock

Nine not to accompany their children to the school? What was he afraid would happen? Do you agree with that decision?

- What role did media play in spreading civil rights information? How would it be different today?
- Reread the section of the book on the Little Rock Nine. Describe how it might have felt to be Elizabeth Eckford.
- In Harlem during the 1950s, laws did not support racial separation, but economic disparity did. What did this mean to blacks and Puerto Ricans living there?
- What role did the Southern Christian Leadership Conference play in the civil rights movement?

Beyond the Book

- Research the life of author James Baldwin. What was his contribution to the civil rights movement?
- How has changing technology influenced the global civil rights movement?
- Who was Daisy Bates? Research her life and discuss her contributions to the civil rights movement.
- Federal and state officials recognized that racism had become the number one American problem. Why was it so difficult to enforce equal rights legislation?
- Imagine that Martin Luther King, Jr. were still alive. What would his role be now?

Books for Further Discussions

Elijah of Buxton by Christopher Paul Curtis. Scholastic, 2007. (CSK Winner, Jane Addams Honor, Newbery Honor)

Malcolm X: By Any Means Necessary by Walter Dean Myers. Scholastic, 1993. (CSK Honor)

The March on Washington by James Haskins. HarperCollins, 1993. (Woodson Winner)

Sugar Changed the World: A Story of Magic, Spice, Slavery, Freedom, and Science by Marc Aronson and Marina Budhos. Clarion, 2010.

Miracle's Boys

By Jacqueline Woodson
N.Y., Putnam, 2000
Grade: 6–9
Genre: Fiction
Core Democratic Value: Pursuit of Happiness
*People have the right to pursue happiness in
their own way, as long as they do not infringe
on the rights of others.*

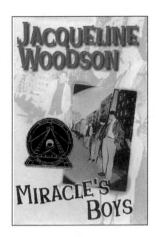

Content Perspective

Jacqueline Woodson demonstrates how the power of unconditional love
and family memories work to keep a fractured family together even after
suffering the tragic loss of both parents. Though guilt and hurt burden
each of the three orphaned brothers, they know in their hearts that they
are there for one another. Memories of parental love and support give
them the strength to confront the emotional pain surrounding their
parents' deaths as they reach out to each other and begin to heal. The
complexity of this family drama is unraveled to reflect the true essence
of family.

Discussion Openers

Students should provide examples of text and/or illustrations to support
their responses.

- Make a list of the adults in the story. In what ways did each one try to
  help the boys after their parents died?
- Each brother has a sense of responsibility about the death of one or
  both of their parents. Discuss those feelings and the impact on the
  boys' lives.
- Illegal and criminal activities play a role in the story. Identify three
  examples and discuss their significance to the plot.
- Who was the man Lafayette described as a "skinny black Santa
  Claus"? Why is he important to the story?
- How did Charlie earn the name Newcharlie?

Beyond the Book

- What knowledge, skills, or character traits did it take for Miracle's boys to carry on without their parents?
- Miracle was an avid reader. She once shared with Lafayette a quote from a book by Toni Morrison: "The function of Freedom, is to free someone else." Research online other quotations about freedom. Make a list to share with your classmates.
- Think about ways to happiness that are available to you, in your life and in your world, that do not step on the rights of others. Record your thoughts in a personal journal.
- Miracle's boys think and talk about being poor in the story. How would you describe what it means to be poor?
- The story reflects a lot on personal and family responsibility. Think about community responsibility. Make a list of five activities or behaviors that reflect community responsibility.

Books for Further Discussions

Forged by Fire by Sharon M. Draper. Atheneum, 1997. (CSK Winner)

Locomotion by Jacqueline Woodson. Putnam, 2003. (CSK Honor)

Ninth Ward by Jewell Parker Rhodes. Little, Brown, 2010. (CSK Honor, Jane Addams Honor)

Tears of a Tiger by Sharon M. Draper. Simon, 1994. (CSK Winner)

Mississippi Challenge

By Mildred Pitts Walter
N.Y., Bradbury, 1992
Grade: 6–9
Genre: Nonfiction
Core Democratic Value: Equality
All citizens have political, social, and economic equality.

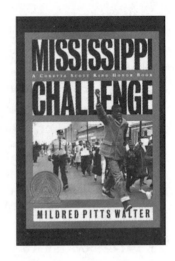

Content Perspective

Mildred Pitts Walter chronicles how black Mississippians won the right to vote after two centuries of denial. Through careful research and contemporary candor the author documents the historical triumphs and failures of citizens who fought and died for justice. The book is a treasury of the early state history of slavery and little-known facts about generations of African American political leaders.

Discussion Openers

Students should provide examples of text and/or illustrations to support their responses.

- What ideas did whites use in the 1900s to justify the statement: "Our public school system is designed primarily for the welfare of the white children of the state, and incidentally for the Negro children"?
- Do you agree with the statement that "fear is the mother of hatred" as it relates to lynching in Mississippi between 1889 and 1940? Why or why not?
- What caused voter registration percentages in Mississippi to rise only 1 percent from 1956 to 1964? What success did the Student Nonviolent Coordinating Committee have in changing those percentages?
- In spite of the possibility that they could lose their jobs or homes for registering to vote, why do you suppose people like Fannie Lou Hamer in Mississippi did it anyway?

- Identify five people who played an active role in the struggle for voting rights in Mississippi. Discuss the impact of their leadership.
- What methods did freedom fighter organizations use to challenge Mississippi laws that disenfranchised black voters?

Beyond the Book

- The following "crimes" were considered justification for hanging a black person: talking disrespectfully, striking a white man, being too prosperous, conjuring. Discuss the difficulty of not committing one of these crimes.
- Describe and discuss voter education classes in 1960 Mississippi.
- Investigate ongoing efforts to disenfranchise voters in post-segregation eras.
- What strategies are used today to ensure that voters are informed about the candidates for office and issues?
- Discuss the impact on American citizens of not having political, social or economic equality.

Books for Further Discussions

Christmas in the Big House, Christmas in the Quarters by Patricia C. McKissack and Fredrick L. McKissack. Scholastic, 1994. (CSK Winner, Orbis Pictus Honor)

Don't Explain: A Song of Billie Holiday by Alexis DeVeaux. Harper & Row, 1980. (CSK Honor)

The Story of Stevie Wonder by James Haskins. Lothrop, Lee and Shepard, 1976. (CSK Winner)

Now Is Your Time! The African-American Struggle for Freedom

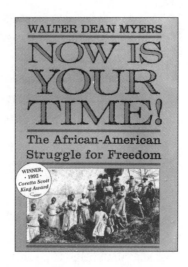

By Walter Dean Myers
N.Y., HarperCollins, 1991
Grade: 6–9
Genre: Nonfiction
Core Democratic Value: Justice
All people should be treated fairly in getting the advantages and disadvantages of our country. No group or person should be favored.

Content Perspective

Walter Dean Myers brings a different perspective to this history of African Americans, which includes a personal anecdotal history of his own family dating back three generations. Of special interest is an aspect of African history seldom included in the history of slavery in the United States. Those times of high culture, noble rulers, great centers of learning, and renowned scholars are chronicled for the reader. Myers takes his title from the call to arms of those who would rise up to fight against the evils of slavery, proclaiming to those in bondage: "Now is your time."

Discussion Openers

Students should provide examples of text and/or illustrations to support their responses.

- How would slavery have been different if plantation owners had allowed the slaves to maintain their culture?
- Enslaved people and indentured servants were treated differently. What accounts for the difference in treatment?
- What perceptions justified the sometimes brutal treatment by Union soldiers of former slaves who joined Union forces?

- Both the Abd al-Rahman Ibrahima enslavement and the Dred Scott case represent significant events in the history of slavery in America. Discuss each as they relate to the ethics of slavery.
- Name three individuals highlighted by Walter Dean Myers and discuss their accomplishments.

Beyond the Book

- Describe three methods enslaved people used to retaliate against their situation.
- What is the fallacy of the justifications used by slaveholders to sell children away from their mothers?
- Reread the introduction. Discuss Myers's selection of the title: *Now Is Your Time!*
- Identify three ways southern loyalists retaliated against blacks after the war.
- Identify three activities former enslaved people engaged in after the war.

Books for Further Discussions

Anthony Burns: The Defeat and Triumph of a Fugitive Slave by Virginia Hamilton. Knopf, 1988. (CSK Honor, Jane Addams Winner)

Rebels Against Slavery: American Slave Revolts by Patricia C. McKissack and Fredrick L. McKissack. Scholastic, 1996. (CSK Honor)

Which Way Freedom? by Joyce Hansen. Walker, 1986. (CSK Honor)

One Crazy Summer

By Rita Williams-Garcia

N.Y., HarperCollins/Amistad, 2010

Grade: 6–12

Genre: Historical Fiction

Core Democratic Value: Life

The individual's right to live should be considered inviolable except in certain highly restricted and extreme circumstances, such as the use of deadly force to protect one's own life or the lives of others.

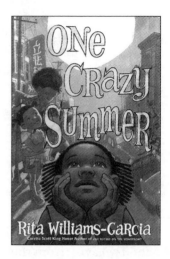

Content Perspective

Eleven-year-old Delphine travels with her two younger sisters, Vonetta and Fern, from Brooklyn to Oakland, California, to visit their estranged mother. It is 1968, and this close-knit threesome spend their days at a summer camp run by the Black Panthers. Williams-Garcia delves honestly into this often-overlooked Panther-sponsored activity. As a piece of historical fiction, *One Crazy Summer* offers a perfect balance between community themes and how they relate to social issues.

Discussion Openers

Students should provide examples of text and/or illustrations to support their responses.

- Find evidence from the text that best describes Delphine's mother. Is she a "Mommy, Mom, or Ma" or a "statement of fact"? How is this related to the role that community sometimes plays in a child's development?
- Keeping in mind that this was 1968, create a character web for Delphine. List character traits and decide if she is believable as an eleven-year-old responsible citizen. Why or why not?
- What do the following statements tell us about the condition of American democracy in 1968: "Power to the people," "Free Huey Newton," "Peace is power, sweet soul sisters," and "We are citizens and we demand respect."

- In the chapter "For the People," Cecile and the Black Panthers discuss the meaning of the word free. How did their viewpoints differ? How were they essentially the same?
- Find passages in the book that best describe Delphine. Would you choose her as a friend? Why or why not?

Beyond the Book

- Create a KWL (what you know, what you want to know, what you learned) chart about the Black Panthers and their role in the civil rights movement.
- Discuss the word endings; -tion, -ism, -actic. How do these endings affect the meaning of a word?
- Research Huey Newton's life. In 1960s Oakland, California, was it possible for him to get a fair trial? Why or why not?
- Choose an illustration from the Coretta Scott King Book Award Illustration Gallery (www.ala.org/emiert/coretta-scott-king-book-awards-illustrations-gallery) that best depicts the core democratic value of the right to live. In a short paragraph explain your choice.
- Explore opportunities in your community to volunteer in a summer camp for younger kids. Create a poster listing these opportunities and post it in your school.

Books for Further Discussions

Monster by Walter Dean Myers. HarperCollins, 1999. (CSK Honor, Printz Winner)

The Rock and the River by Kekla Magoon. Simon & Schuster, 2009. (CSK–John Steptoe Winner)

Shooter by Walter Dean Myers. HarperCollins/Amistad, 2004.

Snitch by Allison Van Diepen. Simon Pulse, 2007.

Yummy: The Last Days of a Southside Shorty by Greg Neri, illus. by Randy DuBurke. Lee & Low, 2010. (CSK Honor)

Rebels Against Slavery: American Slave Revolts

By Patricia C. McKissack and
Fredrick L. McKissack
N.Y., Scholastic, 1996

Grade: 6–9

Genre: Nonfiction

Core Democratic Value: Equality

Everyone should get the same treatment, regardless of race, religion, economic status, or where one's parents or grandparents were born. All people have political, social, and economic equality.

Content Perspective

Stories of the leaders of slave revolts in America leading up to the Civil War account for a great segment of the untold history of our country. The McKissacks' meticulous research reveals the unsung heroes and one-sided reports of slave resistance. The authors go beyond the more commonly known Nat Turner, Harriet Tubman, and John Brown rebels to tell the stories of the Maroons, Denmark Vesey, and Cinque, to name a few. Stories of fearless bravery, guerrilla warfare, and sacrifice for the sake of wives and children trapped in slavery are told in inspirational voices that need to be heard.

Discussion Openers

Students should provide examples of text and/or illustrations to support their responses.

- Slaveholders liked to perpetuate the myth that slaves were happy or at least unaware of any other lifestyle choice. What evidence can be pointed to (other than actual incidents of revolt) that this was far from the truth?
- What were the long-term effects of splitting families by selling wives and children away from spouses and parents?

- Do you think it was wrong for slaveholders to deny slaves opportunities to learn to read? Why or why not?
- What ideas justified the release of the Amistad captives?
- Identify three personality traits that the enslaved heroes and heroines had in common.

Beyond the Book

- What differences, if any, did the ability to read make in the success of a given slave uprising?
- Discuss the reasons white sympathizers gave for supporting slave escapes and/or uprisings.
- How can you justify the idea that some enslaved people became informants for their masters regarding planned escapes and uprisings?
- Trace the origins of the African Methodist Episcopal Church.
- Discuss the reasons for the failure of John Brown's Raid at Harper's Ferry.

Books for Further Discussions

Copper Sun by Sharon Draper. Atheneum, 2006. (CSK Winner)

Now Is Your Time! The African-American Struggle for Freedom by Walter Dean Myers. Scholastic, 1991. (CSK Winner, Woodson Honor, Jane Addams Honor, Orbis Pictus Honor)

Sojourner Truth: Ain't I a Woman by Patricia C. McKissack and Fredrick McKissack. Scholastic, 1992. (CSK Honor)

The Skin I'm In

By Sharon G. Flake
N.Y., Hyperion/Jump at the Sun, 1998
Grade: 6–9
Genre: Fiction
Core Democratic Value: Equality
Everyone should get the same treatment, regardless of race, religion, economic status, or where one's parents or grandparents were born. All people have political, social, and economic equality.

Content Perspective

Weary of the teasing by classmates, Maleeka is determined to make a fresh start in seventh grade by joining the inner circle of the "baddest girls in school." Though the ridicule continues, whether it is her ill-fitting wardrobe or the color of her skin, Maleeka decides it is better to be in the group than to have no friends at all. A new teacher, who possesses a strong aura of confidence along with a blotched complexion, recognizes Maleeka's academic strengths and works to encourage her.

Discussion Openers

Students should provide examples of text and/or illustrations to support their responses.

- What was Maleeka's first reaction to Miss Saunders's skin disorder? How did her perception change over time?
- Given the ill-fitting wardrobe that Maleeka had, what choice would you have made if you were offered the opportunity to wear Charese's hand-me-down clothes?
- Discuss whether it would have been better if Maleeka had shared her negative experiences at school with her mother?
- What evidence can you find to support the description of Miss Saunders as being "serious as a heart attack"?

- Make a list of characters who sincerely care about Maleeka and a second list of people in her life who do not have her best interests at heart. Which list is longer? Why?
- Miss Saunders used several strategies to counteract negative comments about herself and others, including Maleeka. Make a list of the strategies and discuss the effectiveness of each one with your classmates.

Beyond the Book

- Research bullying incidents among youth in your school. What strategies are in place to end this destructive practice?
- Self-discovery through journaling plays an important role in Maleeka's life. Consider starting a personal journal yourself.
- What role does body image play in your school or community?
- Discuss differences among popularity, leadership, and bullying behaviors.
- Research strategies that victims should and should not use to prevent being victimized by bullies.

Books for Further Discussions

The Battle of Jericho by Sharon M. Draper. Atheneum, 2003. (CSK Honor)

Bronx Masquerade by Nikki Grimes. Dial, 2002. (CSK Winner)

I Hadn't Meant to Tell You This by Jacqueline Woodson. Delacorte, 1994. (CSK Honor, Jane Addams Honor)

Jazmin's Notebook by Nikki Grimes. Dial, 1998. (CSK Honor)

Twelve Rounds to Glory: The Story of Muhammad Ali

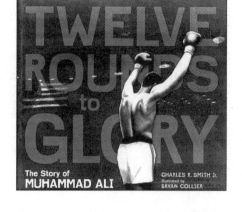

By Charles R. Smith, Jr.,
illus. by Bryan Collier
Cambridge, Candlewick, 2007
Grade: 6–12
Genre: Nonfiction
Core Democratic Value: Liberty

Liberty includes the freedom to believe what you want, to choose your own friends, to have your own ideas and opinions, to express your ideas in public, to meet in groups, and to have any lawful job or business.

Content Perspective

Using freestyle rap poetry, this biography relates the legendary life of boxing champion Muhammad Ali. Like a boxing match, the book is divided into twelve rounds. The book covers his life as Cassius Clay during segregation and his stand against the Vietnam War. His conversion to the Muslim religion, and his new name, changed the way the world looked at this exciting heavyweight champion.

Discussion Openers

Students should provide examples of text and/or illustrations to support their responses.

- What does "Round One" tell you about conditions in the South when Muhammad Ali was born? What effect did this have on his ability to succeed as an athlete?
- When Ali was a boy, his bike was stolen. What does his response tell you about the kind of person he was?
- Read "Round Four" and "Round Six." Ali's language was intense and lively. Do you think Sonny Liston and Joe Frazier were intimidated by Ali's words or actions? Would they intimidate you?

- What impact did Ali's conversion to Islam have on his career as a fighter?
- What does this story tell us about liberty?

Beyond the Book

- Locate the website for Muhammad Ali: www.ali.com/legend_main .php. Click on Rumble in the Jungle. Why was Ali's fight with George Foreman titled Rumble in the Jungle? What does the title imply?
- Watch the video on the website above and write a rap poem about the fight.
- Muhammad Ali's religion is Islam. What do you know about Islam?
- Find a news article about Islam and compare it to what you think you know.
- Identify the Islamic mosque closest to where you live. Make arrangements to interview the imam from that mosque. Compare what you find out with what you thought you knew.

Books for Further Discussions

The Cruisers by Walter Dean Myers. Scholastic, 2010.

We Are the Ship: The Story of Negro League Baseball by Kadir Nelson. Hyperion/Jump at the Sun. (CSK Winner/Honor, Sibert Winner, Orbis Pictus Honor)

The Words of Martin Luther King, Jr., selected by Coretta Scott King, edited by Jean Highland. Newmarket, 1987. (CSK Winner)

We Are the Ship: The Story of Negro League Baseball

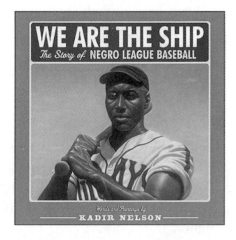

By Kadir Nelson
N.Y., Hyperion/
Jump at the Sun, 2008
Grade: 6–12
Genre: Nonfiction
Core Democratic Value: Justice
All people should be treated fairly in getting the advantages and disadvantages of our country. No group or person should be favored.

Content Perspective

We Are the Ship: The Story of Negro League Baseball is a narrated nonfiction account of the rise and decline of the Negro Leagues. Divided into innings, the book provides information about the beginnings of Negro League baseball, players, managers, and owners. Nelson's dramatic oil paintings and gatefold add to the grace of the story. Realistic images depict players in action on the field, on baseball cards, and in official team portraits. Nelson pays tribute to the unsung heroes of Negro League baseball and highlights an important aspect of American history.

Discussion Openers

Students should provide examples of text and/or illustrations to support their responses.

• Describe the travel conditions that Negro baseball players experienced in the United States. How would you respond to those same travel conditions today?
• Negro League games were described as intense, lively, and entertaining; what impact did this have on the racial makeup of the fans attending?

- The opportunity for Negro League teams to play white teams eventually came in the form of exhibition games. What were the successes of those games? Why didn't they continue?
- Why was the image of African American players so central to the work of Andrew "Rube" Foster in Negro League baseball?
- Once African American baseball players were admitted into National League baseball, how were they treated differently from white players?
- How would National League baseball records of the past be different if African Americans had been included? How would the Baseball Hall of Fame look?
- The success of the Negro League eventually led to Jackie Robinson's signing for the major leagues. How did the success of the Negro Leagues eventually lead to its end?
- What does this story teach us about justice?

Beyond the Book

- Locate the website for The Negro League Baseball Museum: www.nlbm.com/s/index.cfm, click on Negro Leagues History, and discuss the role that Andrew "Rube" Foster played in forming Negro League Baseball.
- Kadir Nelson captures the African American oral tradition on paper. Interview a person who lived during the 1940s and see how his or her life compared to the lives of the players in this book.
- There were two ways of recognizing Negro League players: the National Baseball Hall of Fame and the Major League Hall of Fame. How many Negro League players were finally elected to the National Baseball Hall of Fame? How were they selected to the Major League Hall of Fame? Go to: http://baseballhall.org and click on Hall of Famers.
- Locate and peruse one of the resources listed in the endnotes. Share three interesting facts, truths, or curiosities with your classmates.
- Contrast the way Negro baseball players were treated in Latin America with how they were treated in the United States. Discuss why those differences existed.

Books for Further Discussions

Mare's War by Tanita S. Davis. Knopf, 2009. (CSK Honor)

Somewhere in the Darkness by Walter Dean Myers. Scholastic, 1992. (CSK Honor, Newbery Honor)

Twelve Rounds to Glory: The Story of Muhammad Ali by Charles R. Smith, Jr., illus. by Bryan Collier. Candlewick, 2007. (CSK Honor)

███ **CHAPTER 6** ███

Grades 7–12

Another Way to Dance

By Martha Southgate

N.Y., Delacorte, 1996

Grade: 6–12

Genre: Fiction

Core Democratic Value: Equality

Everyone should get the same treatment, regardless of race, religion, economic status, or where one's parents or grandparents were born.

Content Perspective

Fourteen-year-old Vicki Harris is in love with Mikhail Nikolaievich Baryshnikov. "His friends call him Misha," and so does Vicki, in her dreams. He is a world-famous Russian ballet dancer and a driving force in Vicki's desire to become a ballerina. Vicki is euphoric when she gets a letter of acceptance from New York City's prestigious School of American Ballet (SAB). She is black but has grown up in a mostly white community. This, however, does not prepare her for the racist comments at

CHAPTER 6

Grades 7–12

Another Way to Dance

By Martha Southgate

N.Y., Delacorte, 1996

Grade: 6–12

Genre: Fiction

Core Democratic Value: Equality

Everyone should get the same treatment, regardless of race, religion, economic status, or where one's parents or grandparents were born.

Content Perspective

Fourteen-year-old Vicki Harris is in love with Mikhail Nikolaievich Baryshnikov. "His friends call him Misha," and so does Vicki, in her dreams. He is a world-famous Russian ballet dancer and a driving force in Vicki's desire to become a ballerina. Vicki is euphoric when she gets a letter of acceptance from New York City's prestigious School of American Ballet (SAB). She is black but has grown up in a mostly white community. This, however, does not prepare her for the racist comments at

175

the SAB nor the heartbreaking rebuff from her idol, Misha. With the help of a caring dance instructor and new friends both black and white, Vicki's summer in New York City opens her eyes to myriad possibilities and also to a previously unknown variety of black people living in that thriving city. As her summer unfolds, Vicki develops a broader view of the world in which she lives, and a stronger, more confident sense of her place in it.

Discussion Openers

Students should provide examples of text and/or illustrations to support their responses.

- Up until her summer in New York City, Vicki had only white friends. Do you think her parents chose a good place to raise their black family? Discuss the pros and cons of this decision.
- Vicki meets Michael, a young black man working at a café in New York City. His mother was in the Black Panthers. What did his mother learn from the experience that caused her to forego a career in dance and pursue a law degree?
- What were the effects of people judging Vicki strictly by her skin color?
- What determines Vicki's personal sense of equality, how she is treated, and how she feels about the way she is treated?
- How does Vicki's encounter with Misha shatter her illusions about the dance world?

Beyond the Book

- Watch the movie *Eyes on the Prize* and discuss how it relates to *Another Way to Dance.*
- Why did Vicki's father insist that she and her sister watch the movie *Eyes on the Prize?*
- Research the Black Panther movement and discuss how their ideology might have changed Michael's mother's life.

- On the train and at the SAB Vicki looks for a face like hers. Locate the fiction section of your school or public library. Choose a shelf and count the number of books that represent primarily white characters and the number of books representing persons of color. Discuss your findings.
- Explore opportunities to interact with persons of an ethnicity that differs from your own.

Books for Further Discussions

Bronx Masquerade by Nikki Grimes. Dial, 2002. (CSK Winner)

Harlem Summer by Walter Dean Myers. Scholastic, 2007.

The Land by Mildred D. Taylor. Penguin Putnam/Fogelman, 2001. (CSK Winner)

Monster by Walter Dean Myers. HarperCollins, 2001. (CSK Honor, Printz Winner)

Slam! by Walter Dean Myers. Scholastic, 1996. (CSK Winner)

The Battle of Jericho

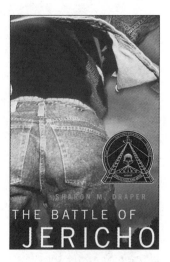

By Sharon M. Draper
N.Y., Atheneum, 2004
Grade: 6–12
Genre: Fiction
Core Democratic Value:
Pursuit of Happiness
People have the right to pursue happiness in their own way, as long as they do not infringe on the rights of others.

Content Perspective

Jericho Prescott knows his future is bright when he is chosen to pledge for an exclusive high school club. Arielle, the most popular girl in the school, becomes very attentive toward him. Jericho is determined to achieve his goal at any cost, even if he has to compromise and give up his dream of attending Julliard. The author vividly captures the voices of contemporary youth while addressing important issues such as peer pressure, bullying, hazing, social acceptance, popularity, and the conflicts about doing the right thing.

Discussion Openers

Students should provide examples of text and/or illustrations to support their responses.

- Identify characters who were profoundly influenced by peer pressure and discuss alternatives to their decisions.
- What kind of person was Jericho? Find evidence of character traits that made him a positive member of the school community and those that might have been less desirable. How might these characteristics have influenced his decisions?
- What aspects of the Warriors of Distinction attracted Josh, Jericho, and Kofi? How does this relate to the pursuit of happiness?
- Jericho was an intelligent, talented high school student. Why didn't he heed Mr. Boston's warning?

- Why did Dana want to join the Warriors of Distinction?
- Identify the adult characters and discuss the role they played in the hazing accident.

Beyond the Book

- November's boyfriend, Josh, dies in a hazing accident. What is the difference between hazing and bullying?
- Create a bullying scenario and dramatize positive interventions.
- Have you ever been asked to do something you know is wrong? Describe the situation. Would you make the same decision again?
- Does your school have a policy regarding hazing or bullying? Discuss the effectiveness of the policy. If it does not have such a policy consider forming a committee to establish one.
- Research online the number of teen deaths in your area. What accounts for the majority of the deaths? Could any of them have been prevented? How?

Books for Further Discussions

Don't Call Me Ishmael by Michael Gerard Bauer. Greenwillow, 2007.

Jumped by Rita Williams-Garcia. Harper Teen, 2009.

Malcolm X: By Any Means Necessary by Walter Dean Myers. Scholastic, 1993. (CSK Honor)

Slam! by Walter Dean Myers. Scholastic, 1996. (CSK Winner)

Stuck on Earth by David Klass. Farrar, Straus and Giroux, 2010.

Because We Are

By Mildred Pitts Walter
N.Y., Lothrop, Lee and Shepard, 1983
Grade: 6–12
Genre: Contemporary Realistic Fiction
Core Democratic Value: Equality
Everyone should get the same treatment,
regardless of race, religion, economic status,
or where one's parents or grandparents
were born.

Content Perspective

Emma Walsh is a senior and honor student at integrated Marlborough High. An unfortunate run-in with one of her teachers sends her back to all-black Manning High, where she struggles with identity issues and school rivalries. A disappointment to her recently divorced parents, Emma takes a proactive stance against a demeaning practice by one of the teachers at Manning and unexpectedly wins the support of fellow classmates. Strong friendships are forged as Emma's intellect and determination bring her senior year to a successful and meaningful conclusion.

Discussion Openers

Students should provide examples of text and/or illustrations to support their responses.

- Why did Emma feel she had to apologize to her friends for her achievements?
- Why did Emma feel she had to prove her blackness?
- Black students congregated in a group during lunch at Marlborough High. Was this by choice? How did students at Manning High divide into groups? Are there any similarities between these two schools?
- Reread the last five paragraphs of chapter 1. What was the difference between what Emma's parents were told in chapter 2 and what really happened?

- Why would Allan choose to go to Manning High when he had many other choices?
- Would you want Marv for a friend? Why or why not? What kind of boyfriend is he?
- A breakdown in communication contributed to Emma's dismissal from Marlborough High. How could Emma's dismissal have been avoided?

Beyond the Book

- How do students divide themselves in your school? On what are these divisions based?
- How do these divisions impact your school experiences?
- How can communication break down with each telling of an event?
- What effect did Emma's transfer to Manning High have on her self-identity?
- Facts are important to understanding an event. What might happen when facts are inaccurate?

Books for Further Discussions

The Battle of Jericho by Sharon Draper. Atheneum, 2003. (CSK Honor)

Becoming Naomi Leon by Pam Muñoz Ryan. Scholastic, 2004. (Pura Belpre Honor)

Slam! by Walter Dean Myers. Scholastic, 1996. (CSK Winner)

The Tequila Worm by Viola Canales. Random House, 2005. (Pura Belpre Winner)

Black Dance in America

By James Haskins
N.Y., Crowell, 1990
Grade: 6–12
Genre: Nonfiction
Core Democratic Value: Diversity
Variety in culture and ethnic background, race, lifestyle, and belief is not only permissible but desirable and beneficial in a pluralist society.

Content Perspective

Extraordinary dancers and creative choreographers successfully navigate racism in America to establish themselves as talented, skilled performers. James Haskins provides intimate details of the struggle for recognition of numerous artists, both the obscure pathfinders and those choreographers and dancers who managed to achieve national and international recognition. This rich volume is a resource for information not necessarily found elsewhere.

Discussion Openers

Students should provide examples of text and/or illustrations to support their responses.

- Discuss the ways in which dances originating in Africa survived in America to become a part of American culture.
- Several dancers adopted nicknames. Identify three such dancers and discuss the origins and reasons for their nicknames.
- Select a dance that became popular in the wider community and discuss how and why that happened.
- Discuss the resistance to black men in ballet as identified by prominent dance critic John Martin.
- Describe one of the dances created by an African American performer.

Beyond the Book

- Black dancers were promoted in unlikely places: Duke University, Ford Foundation, Works Progress Administration. Use the index to research their effect.
- Use the index at the back of the book to make a list of dance companies that promoted black dancers. Select one to research and discuss in detail.
- Select one of the dancers mentioned and describe his or her contribution to dance.
- Discuss the evolution of step dancing and stepping.
- In what ways did the institution of slavery impact dance and dance moves in America?

Books for Further Discussions

Becoming Billie Holiday by Carole Boston Weatherford, illus. by Floyd Cooper. Wordsong, 2008. (CSK Honor)

Flygirl by Sherri L. Smith. Putnam, 2008.

Twelve Rounds to Glory: The Story of Muhammad Ali by Charles R. Smith, Jr., illus. by Bryan Collier. Candlewick, 2007. (CSK Honor)

We Are the Ship: The Story of Negro League Baseball by Kadir Nelson. Hyperion/Jump at the Sun, 2008. (CSK Winner/Honor, Sibert Winner, Orbis Pictus Honor)

Bronx Masquerade

By Nikki Grimes

N.Y., Dial, 2002

Grade: 6–12

Genre: Fiction/Poetry

Core Democratic Value: Diversity

*Variety in culture and ethnic background, race,
lifestyle, and belief is not only permissible but
desirable and beneficial in a pluralist society.*

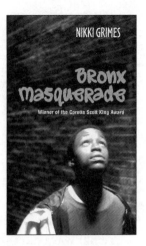

Content Perspective

Eighteen urban youths share their innermost feelings in their class's
open mic poetry presentations. Grimes's characters reveal their identi-
ties and destinies through short monologues paired with self-revealing
poetry. *Bronx Masquerade* offers rich and memorable characters from
diverse backgrounds that not only are on a journey of self-discovery, but
also trying to discover their place in a larger world.

Discussion Openers

Students should provide examples of text and/or illustrations to support
their responses.

- What happens when people let down their guard and invite others to
  share in their stories?
- Was it important for the author to identify Sheila as being white early
  in the story? Why or why not?
- What did we learn about Tyrone as a result of Chankara's first poem?
- What was Raul's motivation for painting?
- How did self-revelation contribute to a new understanding among
  classmates?
- How can the study of the Harlem Renaissance serve as a metaphor for
  Bronx Masquerade?

Beyond the Book

- In *Bronx Masquerade*, the author refers to several Harlem Renaissance poets. Choose one of these poets and research his life to share with your classmates.
- Write a poem, rap, or song about your life or school in a style similar to one of the Harlem Renaissance writers. Then write what you think Tyrone would say about your poem.
- Plan a grade-level poetry slam.
- Diversity comes in many forms: ethnic, cultural, socioeconomic, intellectual, or physical. How does your school address this diversity?
- Locate a news article about real-life bullying among teens. Write a poem about what it might feel like to be the victim.

Books for Further Discussions

After Ever After by Jordan Sonnenblick. Scholastic, 2010. (Schneider Winner)

The Skin I'm In by Sharon G. Flake. Hyperion/Jump at the Sun, 1998. (CSK–John Steptoe Winner)

Who Am I Without Him? by Sharon G. Flake. Hyperion/Jump at the Sun, 2004. (CSK Honor)

Days of Jubilee:
The End of Slavery
in the United States

By Patricia C. and Fredrick L. McKissack

N.Y., Scholastic, 2003

Grade: 6–12

Genre: Nonfiction

Core Democratic Value: Liberty

The right to liberty includes personal freedom, political freedom, and economic freedom.

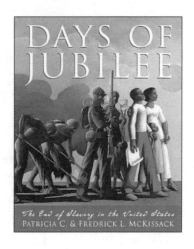

Content Perspective

Abraham Lincoln signed the Emancipation Proclamation on January 1, 1863. The celebration of emancipation, however, took many years because news of the proclamation traveled slowly. The McKissacks carefully chronicle each jubilee that black individuals experienced before the official proclamation and after, bringing to life the people who participated on both sides of this controversial decision. Archival photographs connect faces to events and suggest the role they may have played in bringing an end to the Civil War. Pictures of the carnage displayed in New York at a time when photography was just coming of age provided a front-row view to the realities of this war. A timeline, bibliography, and index enhance the usefulness of the work.

Discussion Openers

Students should provide examples of text and/or illustrations to support their responses.

• Married to a senator, Mary Chestnut was a member of the South Carolina elite. What did she have to lose if slavery was abolished? What might she have gained?

• The Constitution declares that all men are created equal. How then did the Constitution justify slavery?

- Why was it so important for Abraham Lincoln to keep South Carolina in the Union?
- What did the Union stand to lose if all southern states seceded?
- How did the conflict among whites enable some enslaved people to emancipate themselves?
- In his first inaugural speech, Lincoln referred to "persons held to service." Why do you suppose he did not call them slaves?

Beyond the Book

- List twenty words that are synonymous with freedom and jubilee. Create a word search with a partner using these words.
- Research the celebration called Juneteenth and discuss how it relates to Days of Jubilee.
- Locate archival photographs from World War II. What role do photographs play in the telling of that story?
- What can archival photographs tell us that cannot be revealed within a text?
- Research the development of the camera over time. Are today's photographs more or less reliable as documentation of an event?

Books for Further Discussions

Give Me Liberty by L. M. Elliott. Katherine Tegan, 2006.

In Defense of Liberty: The Story of America's Bill of Rights by Russell Freedman. Holiday, 2003. (Orbis Pictus Honor)

The Land by Mildred D. Taylor. Penguin Putnam/Fogelman, 2001. (CSK Winner)

Little Brother by Cory Doctorow. Tom Doherty Associates, 2008.

Long Walk to Freedom: The Autobiography of Nelson Mandela by Nelson Mandela. Little, Brown, 2009.

The Road to Memphis by Mildred D. Taylor. Dial, 1990. (CSK Winner)

Fallen Angels

By Walter Dean Myers
N.Y., Scholastic, 1988
Grade: 7–12
Genre: Fiction
Core Democratic Value: Equality
All citizens have political, social, and economic equality.

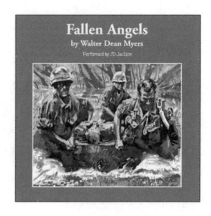

Content Perspective

Seventeen-year-old Richie Perry is intelligent and ambitious, yet faced with limited opportunity. His dilemma: what to do after high school with no money for college. It is 1967, and the Vietnam War is well underway. He enlists with the hope of using the time to get his life together and figure things out. Once in Vietnam, Richie spends his time swatting bugs, tramping through rice paddies, sometimes waist deep, and fighting back the growing terror that becomes more ingrained with each patrol. Using letters to and from home, Myers brings the contradictions of this war to the forefront, as he deftly crafts characters that emerge fully human with all of their frailties and strengths while at the same time successfully refrains from passing judgment. There is just enough "soldier" language in the dialogue to keep the characters real. Some of the depicted atrocities of the war are graphic and not suitable for younger readers.

Discussion Openers

Students should provide examples of text and/or illustrations to support their responses.

- Several times in the story American soldiers are reminded by their commanding officers not to think, just observe and react. Why?
- Name one character trait that you think would be most important for an American soldier serving in the Vietnam War. Explain why.
- What kind of person was Pee-Wee? Would you like him as a friend? Why or why not?

- Why would General Westmoreland have given the order to maximize destruction?
- In this story, American success was measured by the body count of the enemy. What would have been different if it were measured by the body count of Americans?

Beyond the Book

- Use ten sensory words from the story to write a poem about war or what it might have been like to be Perry.
- Father Santora, a Catholic priest, asks, "How come all these places over here have such foreign names?" Discuss the implications of this question.
- Through your local Veteran's Administration, contact a Vietnam War veteran, record the oral history of the soldier's experience, and request permission to deposit it with the Library of Congress.
- Write a letter and send a care package to a military person currently stationed in a war zone.
- Interview a fellow student with a parent in the military. Write a poem in response to that interview.

Books for Further Discussions

1968 by Michael T. Kaufman. Roaring Brook, 2009.

Daniel, Half Human: And the Good Nazi by David Chotjewitz, translated by Doris Orgel. Atheneum, 2004. (Batchelder Honor, Sydney Taylor Honor)

Early Black Reformers by James Tackach, ed. Greenhaven, 2003. (Woodson Winner)

Now Is Your Time! The African-American Struggle for Freedom by Walter Dean Myers. Scholastic, 1991. (CSK Winner, Jane Addams Honor, Woodson Honor, Orbis Pictus Honor)

Sunrise Over Fallujah by Walter Dean Myers. Scholastic Press, 2008.

Forged by Fire

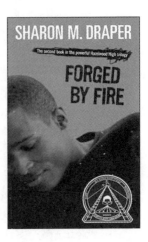

By Sharon M. Draper
N.Y., Atheneum, 1997
Grade: 6–12
Genre: Fiction
Core Democratic Value: Pursuit of Happiness
It is the right of citizens in the United States to pursue happiness in their own way, as long as they do not infringe upon the rights of others.

Content Perspective

Gerald Nickelby discovers two things early on: his mother is unreliable, and playing with fire can be deadly. He is just three years old when left alone in an apartment while his mother is off buying drugs. Bored from lack of adult attention, he discovers the hot thing his mother used to light her cigarettes, and is fascinated by the light as he dances around the apartment. The curtains catch fire and Gerald is left to huddle behind the couch as flames engulf the room. Saved by a neighbor, Gerald is sent to live with his Aunt Queen while his mother serves jail time. These are the best years of his life. Six years later, his mother returns with an abusive husband and Gerald's half sister, Angel. Gerald spends his time at home running interference between Angel and their abusive stepfather. As he realizes that this is no longer a situation he can control, Gerald seeks the help of a friend's father, and that intervention lands the abusive stepfather in jail. Just as tension begins to ease, the stepfather is released and returns to the family. However, he has not reformed and Angel is only saved from his attack by a pot in the kitchen catching fire and a determined brother who dashes in to carry the semiconscious Angel to safety. Draper writes a heart-wrenching story about coming of age under the most difficult of circumstances.

Discussion Openers

Students should provide examples of text and/or illustrations to support their responses.

- What would have happened if Gerald had not told his friend's father about the abuse in the family?
- Gerald and Angel live in an abusive family. What impact might this have on a person's ability to attain happiness?
- Gerald went outside of the family for help. Who else might have been an equally good choice?
- Gerald's stepfather was an abusive man. Why did his mother stay with him?
- How did Gerald's mother's pursuit of happiness affect the happiness of her children?

Beyond the Book

- Identify organizations in your area that work with abused persons, and create a poster for your school with this information.
- Imagine that you are Angel's friend. She has confided in you that her stepfather abuses her. With whom would you share this secret? When is it okay to break a confidence?
- Arrange to have members of your local fire department visit your school to talk about ways to prevent home fires and what to do in case of a fire.
- What makes a hero? Create a story in which you are the hero.
- Have you ever been responsible for caring for a younger child? Write a how-to manual about what works and what does not work in your effort to keep the child safe.

Books for Further Discussions

Bud, Not Buddy by Christopher Paul Curtis. Scholastic, 1999. (CSK Winner, Newbery Winner)

Jumped by Rita Williams-Garcia. Harper Teen, 2009.

Locomotion by Jacqueline Woodson. Putnam, 2003. (CSK Honor)

Stitches by Glen Huser. Groundwood, 2003.

Fortune's Bones: The Manumission Requiem

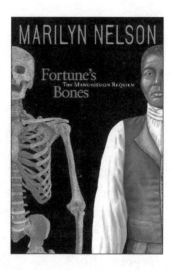

By Marilyn Nelson
N.Y., Front Street, 2004
Grade: 6–12
Genre: Poetry
Core Democratic Value: Liberty
The right to liberty is considered an unalterable aspect of the human condition.

Content Perspective

Six stirring poems commemorate the life of an eighteenth-century enslaved man. His name was Fortune. This requiem by Marilyn Nelson is a lyrical, liturgical remembrance that honors Fortune's life and legacy. In just a few spare pages, Nelson brings Fortune to life with pictorial and literary overlays that allow the reader to see and understand the historical significance of *Fortune's Bones*.

Discussion Openers

Students should provide examples of text and/or illustrations to support their responses.

- Define the term *requiem*. How does Nelson's book balance sadness and joy as depicted in the author's note?
- Reread the third stanza in the poem "Not My Bones." (p. 25) How does the phrase "You can own a man's body, but you can't own his mind" relate to Fortune?
- Scientists, historians, anthropologists, and African American Project Committee members are divided as to whether Fortune's bones should be buried in consecrated ground or kept for future ongoing discoveries. What do you think?
- Think about the mind-set that allowed Fortune's wife to clean the skeleton bones of her husband. Write an imaginary conversation she might have had with herself.

- How does the doctor justify using the bones of his former slave for science? What are the implications of his decision?

Beyond the Book

- Using an anatomy reference tool such as *Gray's Anatomy*, find out how much of the human body is made up of bone, muscle, and water.
- Find a picture of the skeleton of the human hand. How many bones did you discover? Label each one.
- Visit the Mattatuck Museum in Waterbury, Connecticut, online (www.FortuneStory.org). Review the developments of the Fortune project.
- Research skeletons used as teaching tools in medical practice in the 1800s.
- Research the locations of African slave burial grounds other than the one in New York.
- Locate and listen to a recording of a requiem. Respond to the experience.

Books for Further Discussions

Anthony Burns: The Defeat and Triumph of a Fugitive Slave by Virginia Hamilton. Knopf, 1988. (CSK Honor, Jane Addams Winner)

Breaking Ground, Breaking Silence: The Story of New York's African Burial Ground by Joyce Hansen and Gary McGowan. Henry Holt, 1998. (CSK Honor)

The People Could Fly: American Black Folktales by Virginia Hamilton. Henry Holt, 1985. (CSK Winner/Honor)

From the Notebooks of Melanin Sun: A Novel

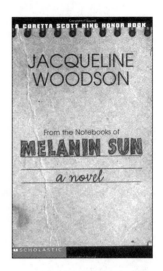

By Jacqueline Woodson

N.Y., Scholastic/Blue Sky, 1995

Grade: 6–12

Genre: Fiction

Core Democratic Value: Equality

Everyone should get the same treatment, regardless of race, religion, gender, economic status, or where one's parents or grandparents were born.

Content Perspective

Thirteen-year-old Melanin Sun lives with his single mom. They are close and share every aspect of their lives—that is, until Mama begins to behave secretively, and Melanin begins to question her suspicious behavior. When rumors start to fly both at school and in the neighborhood, Melanin Sun must confront his biggest fear regarding his mother. Jacqueline Woodson sensitively approaches the subject of what it means to be a lesbian in this tender and sometimes heartbreaking coming-of-age story. Melanin Sun encounters many difficult choices as he works toward acceptance of who his mother is and the realization that she had no more choice in the matter than he had in determining his skin color. Woodson's book includes some sexually explicit language as Melanin experiences changes in his own body.

Discussion Openers

Students should provide examples of text and/or illustrations to support their responses.

- Melanin Sun describes himself as "not a regular boy" and "not slow." What does he mean by this?
- How did Melanin Sun get his name? Why is it important to the story?

- Melanin Sun's perception of lesbians changed over time.
  What accounted for the change?
- The words "faggot" and "faggy" appear frequently in the story,
  used in different ways. Explain the differences.
- How did Melanin feel about white people? Why did he feel that way?
- Why would Melanin and his friends not respond to racial slurs?

Beyond the Book

- Research statistics on teen suicides related to bullying and present
  your findings to classmates.
- Create a list of young adult books that deal with the topic of being gay
  and share the list with your class.
- Explore the possibility of creating GLBT safe zones for students in
  your school with a teacher or school administrator. Are there safe
  zones for other minorities in your school?
- Compile a list of anti-bullying rules for your school and present it to
  school administrators for implementation.
- Create a bullying scenario with the help of other students and your
  teacher. Practice peaceful interventions.

Books for Further Discussions

The Battle of Jericho by Sharon M. Draper. Atheneum, 2003. (CSK
    Honor)

The House You Pass on the Way by Jacqueline Woodson. Delacorte, 1997.

The Last Exit to Normal by Michael Harmon. Knopf, 2008.

So Hard to Say by Alex Sanchez. Simon & Schuster, 2004.

Heart and Soul: The Story of America and African Americans

By Kadir Nelson
N.Y., HarperCollins, 2011
Grade: 6–12
Genre: Nonfiction
Core Democratic Value: Liberty

The right to liberty is considered an unalterable aspect of the human condition. That includes personal freedom, political freedom, and economic freedom.

Content perspective

Author-illustrator Kadir Nelson selected specific historical figures that deepen the understanding of the history of America. The particular role that African American subjects played in the coming-of-age of America provides the focus of this beautifully illustrated title. The inhumane treatment experienced by black Americans in spite of the principles set forth in the Declaration of Independence is the story of the ongoing challenges of the America we know today. Kadir Nelson's presentation provides a personal and intimate perspective of American history that will encourage readers to explore their own family stories.

Discussion Openers

Students should provide examples of text and/or illustrations to support their responses.

- Look at the facial expressions of the portraits in the first four chapters. Describe what might be the thoughts and feelings of the persons depicted in those illustrations.
- What did Jackie Robinson and Rosa Parks have in common?
- What strategies did southerners employ to discourage black Americans from leaving the South?

- In what ways did the South use enslaved people to advance the war before Lincoln signed the Emancipation Proclamation?
- What was the importance of the Mason-Dixon line?

Beyond the Book

- Select one of the black innovators depicted in chapter 10 and research online the significance of his or her innovations.
- Research online the life of Stagecoach Mary (Mary Fields) and her role in the settling of the western territories.
- Explain the role that cities like Detroit played in the Great Migration.
- Research online the events of the Harlem Renaissance. Share three facts of how it did and did not work for African Americans.
- Create a poster that protests an injustice in politics today.

Books for Further Discussions

Elijah of Buxton by Christopher Paul Curtis. Scholastic, 2007. (CSK Winner, Jane Addams Honor, Newbery Honor, Scott O'Dell Winner)

In Defense of Liberty: The Story of America's Bill of Rights by Russell Freedman. Holiday House, 2003. (Orbis Pictus Honor)

Malcolm X: A Graphic Biography by Andrew Helfer, illus. by Randy DuBurke. Hill and Wang, 2006.

M.L.K.: Journey of a King by Tonya Bolden, photography ed. Bob Adelman. Abrams, 2006. (Orbis Pictus Winner)

The Wall: Growing Up Behind the Iron Curtain by Peter Sís. Farrar, Straus and Giroux, 2007. (Orbis Pictus Recommended, Sibert Winner, Caldecott Honor)

Jimi & Me

By Jaime Adoff
N.Y., Hyperion/Jump at the Sun, 2005
Grade: 6–12
Genre: Fiction
Core Democratic Value: Diversity
*Variety in culture and ethnic background, race,
lifestyle, and belief is not only permissible but
desirable and beneficial in a pluralist society.*

Content Perspective

Jimi & Me is a poignant novel written in free verse describing the tumultuous experience of Keith James, a thirteen-year-old, biracial teen who must cope with the unexpected death of his father. Left destitute, Keith and his mother must leave their comfortable life in Brooklyn to share a home with his paternal aunt in a small town in Ohio. Faced with loss, change, and betrayal, Keith finds solace in his music and his idol, Jimi Hendrix.

Discussion Openers

Students should provide examples of text and/or illustrations to support their responses.

- Reread chapter 1. Discuss the difference between feeling angry and acting on that anger. How does it pertain to the protection of life?
- In chapter 1, what did Keith's father mean when he said, "Channel your energy"?
- Find evidence in the text of what Keith's father valued most of all. Do you agree or disagree with his choices? Why or why not?
- Keith found that being a biracial student in his new school in Ohio was even more challenging than he had anticipated. How did his father's words and the words of Jimi Hendrix help him cope with the bullying?
- Find the passage or passages in the book that best tell you about Keith's character and values.

Beyond the Book

- Bullying is an important theme in Jaime Adoff's story. How could you use what Keith learned from his father to intervene in a real-life attempt at bullying in your school?
- Imagine that you are Keith's friend. You have observed that he is depressed. What might you do to support him? With whom would you share your observation?
- Identify community resources available for those suffering from depression and post the information in your school.
- Research the life of Jimi Hendrix. Does he share any character traits with Keith in *Jimi & Me*?
- Listen to the music of Jimi Hendrix and write a response to what you hear.

Books for Further Discussions

The First Part Last by Hope Anita Smith. Simon & Schuster, 2003. (CSK Winner, Printz Winner)

Jumped by Rita Williams-Garcia. Harper Teen, 2009.

Slam! by Walter Dean Myers. Scholastic, 1996. (CSK Winner)

Somewhere in the Darkness by Walter Dean Myers. Scholastic, 1992. (CSK Honor, Newbery Honor)

Stitches by Glen Huser. Groundwood, 2003.

The Way a Door Closes by Hope Anita Smith, illus. by Shane W. Evans. Henry Holt, 2003. (CSK–John Steptoe Winner)

The Land

By Mildred D. Taylor

N.Y., Penguin Putnam/Fogelman, 2001

Grade: 6–12

Genre: Fiction

Core Democratic Value: Liberty

The right to liberty is considered an unalterable aspect of the human condition. This includes personal freedom, political freedom, and economic freedom.

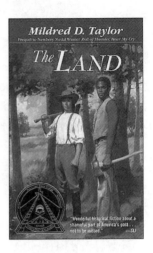

Content Perspective

Paul-Edward Logan was not an ordinary young man. As a child of a mixed race mother and white father, he had privileges other young persons of color did not have during the post–Civil War period. His father, a wealthy Georgia plantation owner, allowed Paul-Edward to sit at his table, as long as there were no guests around. He was taught to read and write, apprenticed as a carpenter, and early on knew nothing about Jim Crow laws. Although Paul-Edward led a privileged life, it did not mean he was equal in the eyes of whites, and it did not mean that his white father would defend him in the presence of other white landowners, or that his closest white brother would not betray him when surrounded by his white friends. These harsh lessons learned, Paul-Edward sets off with his closest friend Mitchell, who is trying to escape his own abusive father, in search of land of his own. Their journey takes them to Mississippi, where life under Jim Crow law proves harsh and unyielding. The two friends separate, each working toward the goal of freedom to live the life he dreamed. Paul-Edward never loses the vision of owning land of his own, a place where he can raise a family without interference from white landowners. This coming-of-age story, based on Mildred D. Taylor's family history, journeys deep into the heart of racism and examines its effect on the right to personal, economic, and political freedom.

Discussion Openers

Students should provide examples of text and/or illustrations to support their responses.

- Which events in Paul-Edward Logan's life do you believe made owning land so important?
- Paul-Edward's daddy wouldn't allow him or his sister Cassie to sit at his table if there were guests present. What would happen if Mr. Logan broke those social rules?
- When Paul-Edward asks Mitchell what he wants out of life, Mitchell replies, "Freedom t'move and freedom t'be." What experiences justify his ideas about freedom?
- Select three incidents or situations that touched you personally and describe how they made you feel.
- What kind of person was Paul-Edward Logan's father?

Beyond the Book

- Research Jim Crow laws and explain how they were allowed to thrive for so long in the South.
- Why was it so difficult for African Americans to purchase land in Mississippi after emancipation?
- Why were southern landowners so devastated by emancipation?
- Land use is an important aspect of land ownership. Observe in your own community how land is used. What effect does land use have on the environment?
- Visit the Environmental Protection Agency website: www.epa.gov and choose from the list of Popular Topics. Share what you discover with your class.

Books for Further Discussions

The Cruisers by Walter Dean Myers. Scholastic, 2010.

Free?: Stories About Human Rights by various authors, for Amnesty International. Candlewick, 2010.

The Heart Calls Home by Joyce Hansen. Walker and Company, 1999.

Sugar Changed the World: A Story of Magic, Spice, Slavery, Freedom, and Science by Marc Aronson and Marina Budhos. Clarion, 2010.

They Called Themselves the K.K.K.: The Birth of an American Terrorist Group by Susan Campbell Bartoletti. Houghton Mifflin Harcourt, 2010.

Lena Horne

By James Haskins
N.Y., Coward-McCann, 1983
Grade: 7–12
Genre: Biography
Core Democratic Value: Liberty
The right to liberty includes personal freedom.

Content Perspective

Lena Horne entered the world of entertainment at the age of sixteen as a last ditch effort to support her family. The tall beautiful teen had been raised mostly by her grandmother while her mother pursued an unsuccessful dream of being in show business. Lena advanced in the world of entertainment, in spite of the racial constrictions of the era, with little talent but with stunning good looks. Her journey to stardom crossed the paths of almost every black entertainer during the 1930s and 1940s. Lena did not escape her mother's overpowering push until her first marriage to Louis Jones, a man she met through her father, Teddy Horne. This marriage produced two children and a spouse who was unsympathetic to the demands of show business. Lena did not realize her personal convictions as a star entertainer until the civil rights movement of the 1960s. Her story is a fascinating account of the actualization of a reluctant star.

Discussion Openers

Students should provide examples of text and/or illustrations to support their responses.

- Discuss the impact of prejudice and discrimination on Lena's early career.
- Describe the role of Brooklyn's black middle class in Lena's life with her grandmother.
- Lena's father was in and out of her life in the early years. Discuss the positives of their relationship.

- Select one of the white performers Lena performed with in her later career. Discuss the circumstances of their collaborations.
- Describe racial identity as it relates to Lena's experiences on Broadway and in Hollywood.

Beyond the Book

- Using the index, identify the following people and their place in the social, intellectual, and political history of black Americans in the United States: Paul Robeson, Walter White, Noble Sissle.
- Discuss elements of the so-called Black Renaissance of the 1960s and 1970s.
- Lena struggled with the label of not being black enough throughout her life. Describe the cumulative effect of black-on-black racism on Lena's personality and career.
- Discuss the controversies surrounding pinups for black soldiers in World War II.
- Discuss the similarities and differences between the singing careers of Lena Horne and Billie Holiday.

Books for Further Discussions

Black Dance in America by James Haskins. Crowell, 1990. (CSK Honor)

Conjure Times: Black Magicians in America by Jim Haskins and Kathleen Benson. Walker & Company, 2001

Twelve Rounds to Glory: The Story of Muhammad Ali by Charles R. Smith, Jr., illus. by Bryan Collier. Candlewick, 2007. (CSK Honor)

We Are the Ship: The Story of Negro League Baseball by Kadir Nelson. Hyperion/Jump at the Sun, 2008. (CSK Winner/Honor, Sibert Winner, Orbis Pictus Honor)

Let the Circle Be Unbroken

By Mildred D. Taylor

N.Y., Puffin, 1981

Grade: 9–12

Genre: Historical Fiction

Core Democratic Value: Justice

People should be treated fairly in the distribution of the benefits and burdens of society.

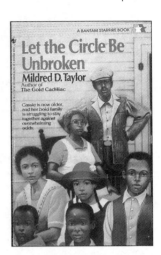

Content Perspective

In this sequel to *Roll of Thunder, Hear My Cry*, Mildred Taylor immerses us further in the Logan family's life as they continue their struggle to keep their land. It is 1934, and the country is simmering in the Great Depression. Agriculture is drying up as farmers fail to pay sharecroppers working their land, and racism runs rampant in this small rural Mississippi town. *Let the Circle Be Unbroken* reveals the uses and abuses of the United States Constitution over time. Taylor brings to life the fear imbedded in the community as threats subtle and not so subtle try to undermine the accomplishments of the Logan family.

Discussion Openers

Students should provide examples of text and/or illustrations to support their responses.

- There was a strong sense of community among black farmers and farm hands. They lived by a certain set of rules, set up mainly to protect themselves from white harassment. What were some of those rules? How would it feel to have to live by them?
- Why was it so important for Stacey, Cassie, Little Man, and Christopher John to attend T.J.'s trial?
- Was it right for Stacey to leave home without telling his family where he was going? Why or why not?

- Would the outcome of Annie Lee's voter registration have been different if Mrs. Logan had stayed with her in the registrar's office? Why or why not?
- The AAA (Agricultural Adjustment Administration) was an attempt by the United States Congress in 1933 to balance supply and demand for farm commodities. What effect did this have on the sharecroppers in *Let the Circle Be Unbroken*?

Beyond the Book

- Research the Voting Rights Act of 1965 and discuss its impact on the civil rights movement.
- Under the American form of democracy, what is the effect of instilling fear in selected groups within the population? How might this impact everyday life?
- Learning the United States Constitution was an important component in Mildred Taylor's story. Why is it just as important in today's world?
- Research and discuss the pros and cons of the Agricultural Adjustment Administration of 1933.
- What role does responsibility play when discussing the United States Constitution?

Books for Further Discussions

The Land by Mildred D. Taylor. Penguin Putnam/Fogelman, 2001. (CSK Winner)

The Road to Memphis by Mildred D. Taylor. (CSK Winner)

Roll of Thunder, Hear My Cry by Mildred D. Taylor. Bantam Books, 1976. (CSK Honor, Jane Addams Honor, Newbery Winner)

To Kill a Mockingbird by Harper Lee. Lippincott, 1960.

Like Sisters on the Homefront

By Rita Williams-Garcia

N.Y., Dutton, 1995

Grade: 6–12

Genre: Fiction

Core Democratic Value: Pursuit of Happiness
It is the right of citizens in the United States to pursue happiness in their own way, as long as they do not infringe upon the rights of others.

Content Perspective

Fourteen-year-old Gayle lives in the projects of New York and is in trouble again. She has a seven-month-old son and is pregnant. When Mama finds out, Gayle loses all rights to pursue her own brand of happiness. First stop is an abortion clinic where Gayle meets a variety of people in a similar situation and discovers that this doesn't only happen to young black girls. Then Mama contacts her estranged brother in the deep South and arranges to send her daughter there in the hope that a household run with an unbreakable set of rules will turn Gayle's life around. In spite of her attempt to manipulate them, Gayle's relatives maintain their good humor. Eventually Gayle allows the chip on her shoulder to fall away, just in time to prevent her cousin, Cookie, from making a terrible mistake. In the end, with the help of Great, Gayle's great-grandmother, Gayle proves that she is made of stronger stuff, and Great bestows on her the responsibility of holding the family history. Strong, sexually explicit language is used briefly to emphasize the importance of words and how they can influence the development of self-esteem.

Discussion Openers

Students should provide examples of text and/or illustrations to support their responses.

- Gayle complained because "everyone was snatching her freedom." What is Gayle's interpretation of freedom? How does it compare to your own?
- Miss Auntie comes flying out of the house when she hears Gayle call her son "stupid." Why was Miss Auntie so angry? Find passages in the story that may have contributed to the way language influenced how Gayle felt about herself.
- What do Gayle's letters to Troy and to Girlfriend say about Gayle and her interpretation of happiness?
- What kind of mother was Gayle? How did Gayle feel about her own mother at the beginning of the story? What made Gayle change her mind?
- Gayle had difficulty adjusting to the rules in her uncle's house. How were these rules different from those in New York? Why are rules important?
- What made Gayle's airplane experience so difficult? What could she have done differently?
- Mama takes Gayle to an abortion clinic. Why was Mama not swayed by the counselor's information about adoption?

Beyond the Book

- Discuss the topic of responsibility as it relates to freedom and the pursuit of happiness.
- What is the difference between happiness and instant gratification?
- Research *Roe v. Wade* and debate for and against its passage.
- Explore options for pregnant teens in your community. Identify similarities and differences in approaches that you discover and discuss the pros and cons with teachers and classmates.
- Read *The First Part Last* by Angela Johnson and compare the main character in that story with Gayle in *Like Sisters on the Homefront*.

Books for Further Discussions

Dear Nobody by Berlie Doherty. Orchard, 1991. (Carnegie Winner)

The First Part Last by Angela Johnson. Simon & Schuster, 2003. (CSK Winner, Printz Winner)

November Blues by Sharon M. Draper. Atheneum, 2007. (CSK Honor)

Someone Like You by Sarah Dessen. Viking, 1998.

Lockdown

By Walter Dean Myers
N.Y., HarperCollins/Amistad, 2010
Grade: 6–12
Genre: Realistic Fiction
Core Democratic Value: Rule of Law
Both the government and the governed should be subject to the law.

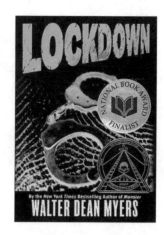

Content Perspective

Author Walter Dean Myers provides a behind-the-scenes view of the juvenile justice system. Lockdown chronicles the plight of fourteen-year-old Reese, incarcerated for a nonviolent offense. The portrayal of Reese and his efforts to stay on the straight and narrow in order to avoid being sent upstate is laced with gritty honesty and the authentic dialogue of those young teens who find themselves trapped in the system. Reese's experience raises the question of who really has to follow the rule of law.

Discussion Openers

Students should provide examples of text and/or illustrations to support their responses.

- Reese commits a victimless crime. Some people believe that there are no victimless crimes. Debate the pros and cons of this position.
- Mr. Hooft makes assumptions about Reese that are not true. How, why, and when does Mr. Hooft's opinion of Reese change?
- In what ways does the system at Progress work to destroy personal initiative, self-determination, and hope in the detainees?
- Discuss the irony of the name of the detention center.
- Identify the role that personal responsibility did or did not play in Reese's life.

Beyond the Book

- Volunteer at a senior citizen center and share your experience with your classmates.
- Walter Dean Myers depicts various protagonists who make mistakes and face consequences much bigger than anticipated. Compare Reese to other main characters in Myers's books.
- Icy, Reese's younger sister, writes a letter to him at Progress that gives him hope for the future. Write a letter of thanks to someone (family member, teacher, clergy) who has encouraged you.
- Locate a news story in your community that involves a juvenile offender. Look for evidence of unintended consequences, personal responsibility, and the rule of law.
- Research juvenile detention facilities in your community. How are they funded?
- Write about a personal relationship you have with a grandparent or other older adult (neighbor, teacher, etc.). Explain the nature of your relationship.

Books for Further Discussions

Maritcha: A Nineteenth-Century American Girl by Tonya Bolden. Harry N. Abrams, 2005. (CSK Honor, Orbis Pictus Recommended)

Mississippi Challenge by Mildred Pitts Walter. Bradbury, 1992. (CSK Honor)

Monster by Walter Dean Myers, illus. by Christopher Myers. Harper-Collins, 1999. (CSK Honor, Printz Winner)

The Road to Memphis by Mildred D. Taylor. Dial, 1990. (CSK Winner)

Roll of Thunder, Hear My Cry by Mildred D. Taylor. Dial, 1976. (CSK Honor, Newbery Winner, Jane Addams Honor)

Maritcha: A Nineteenth-Century American Girl

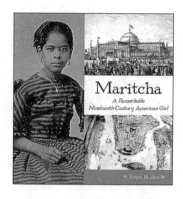

By Tonya Bolden

N.Y., Harry N. Abrams, 2005

Grade: 6–12

Genre: Nonfiction

Core Democratic Value: Justice

All people should be treated fairly in getting the advantages and disadvantages of our country. No group or person should be favored.

Content Perspective

"Aim high! Stand tall! Be strong!" and "Do!" are the opening words of Tonya Bolden's *Maritcha: A Nineteenth-Century American Girl*. Based on Maritcha Remond Lyons's eighty-one-page memoir, this beautifully crafted book describes the life of the daughter of a middle-class free black family living in New York City in the mid-1800s. Racial riots, sparked by demonstrations against the new draft laws, drove the Lyons family from their home. Despite the many hardships that resulted, Maritcha graduated as the first black student from the local high school in her new home state of Connecticut. She truly stood tall. Illustrated with archival photographs and drawings, Bolden's book brings to life a troubling time in United States history. Endnotes and a selected bibliography offer opportunities for further research.

Discussion Openers

Students should provide examples of text and/or illustrations to support their responses.

- Slavery ended in New York State in 1827, yet Marticha and her family were driven from their home in 1863. As free-born citizens, why couldn't Maritcha's family participate equally in New York society?
- Explain why prowar politicians, rich people, abolitionists, and blacks were all targets of the rioters.
- Why did people in 1863 oppose the draft?

- Is there any other time in history when there were protests against the draft? When? Why? How were they the same as the riots in 1863? How were they different?
- Use Maritcha's story to explain what happens when a society falls into chaos. How does the social structure change? What are some implications of those changes?

Beyond the Book

- Go to the New York Public Library Digital Gallery: http://history 1800s.about.com/gi/o.htm?zi=1/XJ&zTi=1&sdn=history1800s&cdn =education&tm=58&f=00&tt=33&bt=0&bts=0&zu=http%3A// digitalgallery.nypl.org/. In the More Options search box, type in draft riots. Select an image and write a newspaper article about what is happening in that picture.
- Debate the pros and cons of violent versus nonviolent protest.
- Compare and contrast Nelson Mandela's approach to conflict with that of Malcolm X. Explain how they are different and how they might be the same.
- Initiate the formation of a conflict resolution committee at your school. How might the core democratic value of justice be included?
- Choose a civil rights leader who embodies the core democratic value of justice. Explain your choice.

Books for Further Discussions

Long Walk to Freedom: The Autobiography of Nelson Mandela by Nelson Mandela. Little, Brown, 2009.

Malcolm X: By Any Means Necessary by Walter Dean Myers. Scholastic, 1993. (CSK Honor)

Twelve Rounds to Glory: The Story of Muhammad Ali by Charles R. Smith, Jr., illus. by Bryan Collier. Candlewick, 2007. (CSK Honor)

We Are the Ship: The Story of Negro League Baseball by Kadir Nelson. Hyperion/Jump at the Sun, 2008. (CSK Winner/Honor, Orbis Pictus Honor, Sibert Winner)

November Blues

By Sharon M. Draper

N.Y., Atheneum, 2007

Grade: 6–12

Genre: Fiction

Core Democratic Value: Pursuit of Happiness
People have the right to pursue happiness in their own way, as long as they do not infringe on the rights of others.

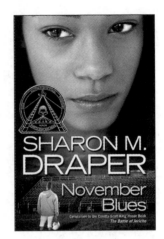

Content Perspective

Sixteen-year-old November is a popular high school girl with scholarship offers. Her boyfriend, Josh, died in a hazing accident. Now she learns she is pregnant with his child, and Josh's parents want the baby. As November sorts through the difficult decisions she must make, she has the support of friends, and the reluctant acceptance of her mother. While she wrestles with the challenges her pregnancy presents, she discovers that her baby may have problems, and as her body changes, so does her life. The reality of responsible parenthood looms larger and larger, the decisions become more and more complicated.

Discussion Openers

Students should provide examples of text and/or illustrations to support their responses.

- In chapter 4, November recalled the role that news commentators played immediately following Josh's death. Discuss the role that reporters play in creating news.
- What kind of boy was Josh? Find evidence of character traits that made him a positive member of the school community and those that might have been less desirable. What role did these characteristics play in his demise?
- Is there a relationship between peer pressure and bullying? Find examples of each in the story.

- What does this story tell us about the pursuit of happiness? Discuss Logan and Arielle's behavior toward Olivia within this context.
- Find passages in the story that best describe November's character. Would you choose her as a friend? Why or why not?

Beyond the Book

- Do you believe that teens are prepared for the responsibilities of parenthood? Why or why not?
- Calculate what the cost for a baby would be for one week. Include baby bottles, baby food, wipes, pacifiers, diapers, clothes, car seat, blankets, etc.
- November's boyfriend, Josh, died in a hazing accident. What is the difference between hazing and bullying?
- Create a bullying scenario and dramatize positive interventions.
- Does your school have an anti-bullying policy? Discuss what should be included in the policy.

Books for Further Discussions

Don't Call Me Ishmael by Michael Gerard Bauer. Greenwillow, 2007.

Jumped by Rita Williams-Garcia. Harper Teen, 2009.

Malcolm X: By Any Means Necessary by Walter Dean Myers. Scholastic, 1993. (CSK Honor)

Slam! by Walter Dean Myers. Scholastic, 1996. (CSK Winner)

Stuck on Earth by David Klass. Farrar, Straus and Giroux, 2010.

The Other Side: Shorter Poems

By Angela Johnson
N.Y., Orchard Books, 1998
Grade: 6–12
Genre: Poetry/Nonfiction
Core Democratic Value: Pursuit of Happiness
It is the right of citizens in the United States to pursue happiness in their own way, as long as they do not infringe upon the rights of others.

Content Perspective

Shorter is not the length of a poem but a town in Alabama in the process of being dismantled and turned into a dog track. Author Angela Johnson's history is there, and Grandmama summons her back to the place she both loved and hated. Welcomed by music from a cassette player pouring out of a house that has not yet been boarded up, the narrator begins her journey back in time, from the disaster of early piano lessons to talks of war: "Wars with bombs/ Wars with swords/ Even wars with aliens." The result was the breaking of all the windows at an army recruiting office in Birmingham. Johnson's story in poetic form introduces the variety of characters living in Shorter, from Grandmama to a member of the Black Panthers "Who could stare down a killer," to her Daddy with his Vietnam nightmares. Johnson demonstrates how characters and events from the past can contribute to one's developing sense of self.

Discussion Openers

Students should provide examples of text and/or illustrations to support their responses.

- Reread the poem "War." What caused Harper Crew to break all the windows at the army recruiting office in Birmingham?

- Refer to the poem "Country Girl" and discuss ideas that justify her anger with the world.
- In the poem "Where You Been," Grandmama says that where you have been is more important than where you are going. Do you agree with her? Why or why not?
- Reread the poem "Nineties." What effect might the white child's words have had on the black girl in the car?
- Find the passages in the text that best describe the kind of person that Grandmama was.
- Why is this book titled *The Other Side*? If you could choose a title, what would it be?

Beyond the Book

- The cousin with country ways was mad at the world. She had joined the Black Panthers. Research the Black Panthers and discuss the pros and cons of membership.
- On February 1, 1960, four African American students sat at an all-white lunch counter. What were they protesting? What made this protest unique? Go to www.northcarolinahistory.org/encyclopedia /299/entry for details.
- Grandmama was so opposed to the girls smoking that she took measures to ensure they would never smoke again. Research the dangers of cigarette smoking. Plan an informational event with classmates at your school.
- When the country cousin became angry, she joined the Black Panthers. When Harper Crew became angry, he broke windows. Can you think of more constructive ways to deal with anger?
- Check out the Mayo Clinic Anger Management website: www.mayo clinic.com/health/anger-management/MH00102 for 10 tips for managing anger.

Books for Further Discussions

Freedom Songs by Yvette Moore. Orchard Books, 1991.

Jimi & Me by Jaime Adoff. Hyperion/Jump at the Sun, 2005. (CSK Winner)

Like Sisters on the Homefront by Rita Williams-Garcia. Dutton, 1995. (CSK Honor)

Mare's War by Tanita S. Davis. Knopf, 2009. (CSK Honor)

Power to the People: The Rise and Fall of the Black Panther Party by Jim Haskins. Simon & Schuster, 1997.

Rainbow Jordan

By Alice Childress
N.Y., Putnam, 1981
Grade: 7–12
Genre: Contemporary Realistic Fiction
Core Democratic Value: Pursuit of Happiness
It is the right of citizens in the United States to
pursue happiness in their own way, as long as
they do not infringe upon the rights of others.

Content Perspective

More than the typical teen angst, Rainbow Jordan's life demands constant negotiation of the pitfalls of life without the guidance of a parent. Rainey, as she prefers to be called, employs carefully scripted deception to avoid placement in an interim foster home, an effort at which she regularly fails. Not wanting to "out" her absent mother is her primary goal. Although her success in deceiving school authorities is eventually thwarted, Rainey's steadfast loyalty reflects both her devotion to her mother and her ability to survive the ups and downs of the adult world.

Discussion Openers

Students should provide examples of text and/or illustrations to support their responses.

- List the adult women in Rainbow's life. Discuss the role each one played in Rainbow's world.
- Is it ever okay to tell a lie? Why or why not?
- What did Rainbow think of her given name?
- Identify ways that Rainbow's boyfriend influenced her life.
- Many adults are offended by the salty language used by the characters in the book. Why do you suppose the author, Alice Childress, included it?

Beyond the Book

- What other titles are you familiar with in which a character must hide behind untruths to survive in an adult world?
- Discuss the impact of becoming a mother at fifteen in the world as you know it. Is it the same or different for fathers?
- Create a new design for a paperback cover of *Rainbow Jordan*.
- Investigate the process of becoming a foster child. When, why, and how does it happen?
- What role do education and life experience play in establishing a stable lifestyle?

Books for Further Discussions

Forged by Fire by Sharon M. Draper. Atheneum, 1997. (CSK Winner)

A Hero Ain't Nothin' but a Sandwich by Alice Childress. Coward, McCann & Georghegan, 1973. (CSK Honor, Jane Addams Honor)

Sweet Whispers, Brother Rush by Virginia Hamilton. Philomel, 1982 (CSK Winner, Newbery Honor)

Tears of a Tiger by Sharon M. Draper. Atheneum, 1994. (CSK–John Steptoe Winner)

The Tequila Worm by Viola Canales. Wendy Lamb, 2005. (Pura Belpre Winner)

The Road to Memphis

By Mildred D. Taylor
N.Y., Dial, 1990
Grade: 6–12
Genre: Fiction
Core Democratic Value: Equality

All citizens have political, legal, social, and economic equality. Extreme economic inequality tends to undermine all other forms of equality and should therefore be avoided.

Content Perspective

Cassie is a senior in high school, living in Mississippi, dreaming of college and a career as a lawyer. It is 1941, with war looming on the horizon and Jim Crow laws deeply embedded in the South. Evil lurks around every corner for black people in Cassie's town, and when a black young man retaliates for the abuse, he is on the run for his life. Family and friends, both black and white, help in the escape, but not until Cassie suffers a humiliation that will live with her for the rest of her life. Mildred Taylor brings characters and events to life with her rich language and mesmerizing storytelling ability.

Discussion Openers

Students should provide examples of text and/or illustrations to support their responses.

- There are subtle ways of making people feel inferior. Why did Cassie's parents forbid her to go into the Wallaces' store?
- Everyone was proud of Uncle Hammer's new Packard. Examine the text for evidence of the importance of a car. What did it symbolize?
- There were rules about blacks and whites riding in cars together. What were they? What was the purpose of these rules?
- When Jeremy wanted to ride in Stacey's car, Stacey hesitated. Why?

- Cassie, Moe, and their friends called Jeremy by his first name, but only when no other whites were present. What would have happened if they had broken this social rule?
- What kind of person was Jeremy? Would you want him for a friend? Why or why not?

Beyond the Book

- Compare the actions of the white boys in *The Road to Memphis* with those of modern-day terrorists. How are they the same? How are they different?
- Research sharecropping. What were the rules regarding black sharecroppers? What purpose did these rules serve?
- Learn more about *Plessy v. Ferguson* and the separate but equal law at: www.pbs.org/wnet/jimcrow/stories_events_plessy.html. Justice John Harlan was the lone dissenter. What was his argument?
- Who was Mary Church Terrell? What role did she play in the civil rights movement?
- Visit the Ferris State University Jim Crow Museum of Racist Memorabilia online at: www.ferris.edu/jimcrow/what.htm. Discuss ways that this exhibit can promote a better understanding of racial injustice.

Books for Further Discussions

Copper Sun by Sharon M. Draper. Atheneum, 2006. (CSK Winner)

The Land by Mildred D. Taylor. Penguin Putnam/Fogelman, 2001. (CSK Winner)

Like Sisters on the Homefront by Rita Williams-Garcia. Dutton, 1995. (CSK Honor)

Roll of Thunder, Hear My Cry by Mildred D. Taylor. Dial, 1976. (CSK Honor, Newbery Winner, Jane Addams Honor)

The Rock and the River

By Kekla Magoon
N.Y., Simon & Schuster, 2009
Grade: 6–12
Genre: Historical Fiction
Core Democratic Value: Life
The individual's right to live should be considered inviolable except in certain highly restricted and extreme circumstances, such as the use of deadly force to protect one's own life or the lives of others.

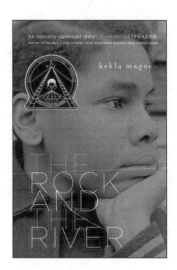

Content Perspective

Thirteen-year-old Sam lives in a middle-class neighborhood with his mother, father, and older brother, Stick, just blocks away from the projects of Chicago. It is 1968. Living with a father who is a friend of Martin Luther King, Jr., as well as a civil rights leader with a large following of his own, means that Sam is well acquainted with civil rights marches and peaceful demonstrations. When he discovers his brother's secret life, however, Sam realizes there is more than one way to challenge racism: his father's way of passive resistance or the more confrontational approach of the Black Panther Party. Thinking he must choose between these two factions, he realizes that his brother is a community organizer, making improvements in the neighborhood through his connections with the Black Panthers. Sam gains a richer understanding of both Panther and pacifist. Meanwhile, Sam's father confronts his own biases regarding the Black Panthers and emerges with a fuller understanding of his sons' desire to overcome the racist injustices that they experience every day.

Discussion Openers

Students should provide examples of text and/or illustrations to support their responses.

- When Sam goes into the hospital gift shop, the salesperson treats him abusively, calling him a thief and using racist language. Why didn't Sam tell his father what happened in the store?
- There were several people watching when the police attacked Bucky in broad daylight. Why did no one come to his rescue?
- Black parents instructed their teens never to run when they were in public. Explain Sam's statement, "The cops see a brother running at night, they pick him up for sure."
- Sam's parents wanted to know where he was and who he was with at all times. Why were they so strict?
- Identify passages in the text that best describe Sam. What kind of person is he?

Beyond the Book

- Even today, why might black men and boys fear police? Research current news articles that support this premise.
- What does it mean to be tried by a jury of your peers?
- Who were Huey Newton and Bobby Seale? Write an essay discussing their philosophy regarding civil rights.
- Research civil rights lawyers Clive Billings and Eric Richman and discuss their role in the civil rights movement.
- Explore the community service activities of the Black Panther Party.

Books for Further Discussions

Monster by Walter Dean Myers. HarperCollins, 1999. (CSK Honor, Printz Winner)

One Crazy Summer by Rita Williams-Garcia. HarperCollins/Amistad, 2010. (CSK Winner, Newbery Honor)

Shooter by Walter Dean Myers. HarperCollins/Amistad, 2004.

Snitch by Allison Van Diepen. Simon Pulse, 2007.

Yummy: The Last Days of a Southside Shorty by Greg Neri, illus. by Randy DuBurke. Lee & Low, 2010. (CSK Honor)

Somewhere in the Darkness

By Walter Dean Myers

N.Y., Scholastic, 1992

Grade: 6–12

Genre: Fiction

Core Democratic Value: Equality

Everyone should get the same treatment, regardless of race, religion, economic status, or where one's parents or grandparents were born.

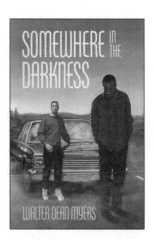

Content Perspective

A road trip from New York to Memphis introduces Jimmy Little to his father's life. Crab Little recently walked away from prison in search of his son, now living in a rundown apartment building with Mama Jean, a hard-working, caring custodial adult. Jimmy is in tenth grade and doing well in school when his father shows up, with two goals in mind: to convince his son that he is not a murderer, and to give his son a chance to know him as a father. It does not take Jimmy long to discover that Crab is seriously ill and that he is constantly looking over his shoulder for police he is sure are searching for him. Memories of his life with Mama Jean keep Jimmy anchored as his father's life unfolds around him, and what he learns about life and family relationships will serve him well into the future.

Discussion Openers

Students should provide examples of text and/or illustrations to support their responses.

- New York is very different from rural Tennessee. Explain some of the differences.
- What if Jimmy had declined his father's invitation to join him on his journey back home? What did he have to gain? What did he stand to lose?
- What kind of person was Crab? Would you like him as a friend? Why or why not?

- How was Crab treated when he was arrested for the crime he said he didn't commit? Is there a possible connection between the way he was treated and the illness that finally kills him?
- Who was Mama Jean? How did she fit into Jimmy's life?

Beyond the Book

- Investigate Jim Crow laws using this website: http://academic .udayton.edu/race/02rights/jcrow02.htm. Select one of the Jim Crow laws from Tennessee and discuss how this law might have affected Crab's life.
- Explore definitions of conjurer and healer in various cultures. Interview a grandparent or other older family member regarding a possible conjurer or healer in his or her life. Why might someone choose alternative medicine over traditional medical treatment?
- There is evidence that the number of incarcerated whites is inordinately lower than the number of incarcerated people of color. Using Crab as an example, what might account for this discrepancy?
- Observe student activities in your school. Are all students treated the same? Provide examples.
- Who is your primary caregiver? List the qualities that make that caregiver special.

Books for Further Discussions

Daniel, Half Human: And the Good Nazi by David Chotjewitz, translated by Doris Orgel. Atheneum, 2004. (Batchelder Honor, Sydney Taylor Honor)

The Land by Mildred D. Taylor. Penguin Putnam/Fogelman, 2001. (CSK Winner)

Roll of Thunder, Hear My Cry by Mildred D. Taylor. Dial, 1976. (CSK Honor, Jane Addams Honor, Newbery Winner)

Slam! by Walter Dean Myers. Scholastic, 1996. (CSK Winner)

The Watson's Go to Birmingham—1963 by Christopher Paul Curtis. Delacorte, 1995. (CSK Honor, Jane Addam Honors, Newbery Honor)

Sweet Whispers, Brother Rush

By Virginia Hamilton
N.Y., Philomel, 1982
Grade: 6–12
Genre: Fiction
Core Democratic Value: Life
The individual's right to live should be considered inviolable.

Content Perspective

Left to care for her mentally challenged brother, Dabney, while her mother works far away from home, fourteen-year-old Teresa, called Tree by her friends, encounters the ghost of her long-dead uncle, Brother Rush. This strange but realistic meeting changes the way Tree views her absent mother and her family history.

Discussion Openers

Students should provide examples of text and/or illustrations to support their responses.

- Choose three descriptive words that characterize Tree.
- What safeguards did Vy leave in place to support and protect Tree and Dab while she worked away from home? Were the safeguards sufficient? Why or why not?
- Tree became skilled at being evasive with school authorities regarding the circumstances of her life at home. When and why does her evasiveness fall apart?
- Discuss the meals Tree prepared for herself and Dab. What simple meals can you prepare?
- Were you surprised at the role Miss Pricherd came to play in Tree's life? Why or why not?

Beyond the Book

- What does the reader discover about Brother Rush's style of dress? Create a drawing or magazine cutout of Brother Rush's stylish wardrobe.
- Research the legal age and circumstances under which a parent can leave a child home alone.
- Is porphyria a real disease or condition? Investigate the characteristics of porphyria online.
- How did Silversmith get his nickname? Create a nickname for yourself or a very close friend or family member. Explain how the nickname fits.
- Read the book *Rainbow Jordan* by Alice Childress. Compare the lives of Tree and Rainey.

Books for Further Discussions

A Hero Ain't Nothin' but a Sandwich by Alice Childress. Coward, McCann & Georghegan, 1973. (CSK Honor, Jane Addams Honor)

Rainbow Jordan by Alice Childress. N.Y., Putnam, 1981. (CSK Honor)

The Tequila Worm by Viola Canales. Wendy Lamb, 2005. (Pura Belpre Winner)

Toning the Sweep by Angela Johnson. Orchard, 1993. (CSK Winner)

Trouble's Child

By Mildred Pitts Walter
N.Y., Lothrop, Lee and Shepard, 1985
Grade: 6–12
Genre: Fiction
Core Democratic Value: Pursuit of Happiness
It is the right of citizens in the United States to pursue happiness in their own way, as long as they do not infringe upon the rights of others.

Content Perspective

Thirteen-year-old Martha lives with her grandmother, Titay, on an island in Louisiana. Steeped in superstition, island rules are of paramount importance, and everyone must abide by them or suffer the consequences. The island requires Martha, who is about to turn fourteen, to begin thinking about marriage. Martha, however, has other plans. She wants to leave the island with all of its fears behind and pursue an education elsewhere. When a handsome young stranger washes up on the beach, she sees a possible means of escape. Martha encounters many challenges along the way. Torn between loyalty to her grandmother, who wants her to follow in her footsteps and become the island midwife-healer, and her strong desire to expand her world, Martha struggles to find a way. First, she must win over her grandmother. Then she must convince islanders that what she wants to do is not evil. Mildred Pitts Walter deftly pulls all of these threads together as she weaves a tale of adventure, the power of fear, and the possibilities of deliverance.

Discussion Openers

Students should provide examples of text and/or illustrations to support their responses.

• Titay was disappointed when Martha called her teacher by her first name. Why did Martha's behavior upset the islanders?

- Everyone on the island agreed to abide by a strict set of rules. What was the purpose of these rules?
- Is it ever okay not to follow rules?
- Did Blue Isle function like a democracy? Why or why not?
- Who had the most power on the island? Provide evidence.

Beyond the Book

- Discuss the relationship between responsibility and freedom.
- List superstitions that are prevalent today. Discuss their origins.
- Compare the differences and similarities between folk practices and superstition.
- What purpose do superstitions serve?
- Everyone is entitled to pursue happiness in his or her own way. What responsibilities accompany that right? Provide examples.

Books for Further Discussions

The First Part Last by Angela Johnson, Simon & Schuster, 2003. (CSK Winner, Printz Winner)

Jumped by Rita Williams-Garcia. Harper Teen, 2009.

Like Sisters on the Homefront by Rita Williams-Garcia. Dutton, 1995. (CSK Honor)

Miracle's Boys by Jacqueline Woodson, Putnam, 2000. (CSK Winner)

Somewhere in the Darkness by Walter Dean Myers. Scholastic, 1992. (CSK Honor, Newbery Honor)

Yummy:
The Last Days of
a Southside Shorty

By Greg Neri,
illus. by Randy DuBurke
N.Y., Lee & Low, 2010
Grade: 6–12
Genre: Nonfiction/Biography/
Graphic Novel
Core Democratic Value: Life

*The individual's right to live should be
considered inviolable except in certain
highly restricted and extreme circumstances.*

Content Perspective

Robert Sandifer lived on the South Side of Chicago in 1994. That is, until
he was eleven years old. Then his life ended. How does eleven-year-old
Robert (Yummy because he is known for his sweet tooth) become a killer
and then a corpse in the blink of an eye? Yummy lives with his grandmother, who is also responsible for twenty other children ranging in age
from toddler to teen. She takes in cast-off children from various family members, including Yummy's drug-addicted mother, but is under-
standably overwhelmed and unable to account for every child every day.
She does the best she can under her current circumstances, yet Yummy
slips through the cracks. He desperately wants to belong somewhere,
anywhere. When he is on the street, he sees how gang members hang
together, watch out for each other. He sets a goal to become one of them.
They give him high fives, pats on the back, and the gift of a gun. He feels
important, welcome. There is a catch, however; he has to prove himself
"man" enough. Given the size of the gun and the size of the boy, his aim
is not steady, and he shoots and kills fourteen-year-old Shavon Dean,
an innocent bystander. He thinks the gang will protect him, but instead
they kill him, leaving his body under a dark and lonely bridge. Randy

DuBurke's stark black-and-white illustrations bring Robert Sandifer's life into focus in this short graphic biography of an eleven-year-old boy. Is he killer or victim?

Discussion Openers

Students should provide examples of text and/or illustrations to support their responses.

- At the bottom of page 19 there is a picture of a teacher in front of a classroom with many empty desks. Explain.
- Imagine that you are Robert. What does it feel like?
- Look carefully at the illustrations on pages 10 and 11. What do they tell you about the neighborhood?
- Why did Yummy choose to join the Black Disciples?
- Why did people in the neighborhood feel helpless about gang activities?

Beyond the Book

- Create an autobiography in graphic novel format about your first eleven years. Compare your experiences to Robert's.
- Gang members generally do not own property or pay taxes in the areas that they try to rule. In what are they investing their efforts?
- Investigate local neighborhood watch teams. Discuss the pros and cons of these groups.
- What role does community involvement play in eradicating gang activities? Support your ideas with online journal and newspaper articles.
- If each person has the right to protect his or her life under the U.S. Constitution and the Bill of Rights, what accounts for the lack of respect for life as demonstrated in this biography?

Books for Further Discussions

Harlem Hustle by Janet McDonald. Farrar, Straus and Giroux, 2006.

If I Grow Up by Todd Strasser. Simon & Schuster, 2009.

Monster by Walter Dean Myers. HarperCollins, 1999. (CSK Honor, Printz Winner)

The Rock and the River by Kekla Magoon. Simon & Schuster, 2009. (CSK–John Steptoe Winner)

Shooter by Walter Dean Myers. HarperCollins/Amistad, 2004.

Snitch by Allison Van Diepen. Simon Pulse, 2007.

A Wreath for Emmet Till by Marilyn Nelson. Houghton Mifflin, 2005. (CSK Honor, Printz Honor).

CHAPTER 7

Grades 9–12

Copper Sun

By Sharon M. Draper
N.Y., Atheneum, 2006
Grade: 9–12
Genre: Historical Fiction
Core Democratic Value: Liberty
The individual's right to liberty is considered an unalterable aspect of the human condition.

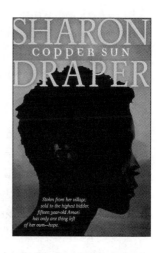

Content Perspective

Fifteen-year-old Amari's struggle with the evils of slavery is a historical reality check for today's young adult readers. Dragged from her African home, forced onto a slave ship, and purchased as a gift for a plantation owner's son, Amari held a growing belief that the evil cruelties of slavery were pervasive and any possibility of change unthinkable. The impending sale of the cook's son hastened the necessity to flee. Forming an unlikely alliance with an indentured servant, the threesome sets off on a treacherous journey of hope and survival.

Discussion Openers

Students should provide examples of text and/or illustrations to support their responses.

- Prior to her abduction Amari lived in a society that believed in community strength and personal worth. How did Amari carry these values to America?
- Polly was an indentured servant. Explain what it means to be an indentured servant. In what ways is Polly's story both similar to and different from Amari's?
- Amari and Polly struggled with their unlikely friendship. How would the outcome have changed if they did not have a trusting relationship?
- Historical evidence and common wisdom dictated that enslaved Africans would flee north toward freedom. Do you agree with Amari's decision to travel south in their pursuit of freedom?
- Using evidence from the story, support the idea that Amari provided responsible leadership on the flight toward freedom.

Beyond the Book

- Research information resources on black settlements in the United States. In which regions of the country are they located?
- In what ways did the emancipation of the enslaved affect the relationship between slaveholders and newly freed slaves?
- Research the practice of indentured servitude. Share your findings with your classmates.
- Research modern St. Augustine, Florida. What evidence can you find that it was once a haven for escaped slaves?
- The work that enslaved people were required to do was often described as backbreaking. Discuss reasons that they were able to endure and survive.

Books for Further Discussions

Day of Tears by Julius Lester. Hyperion/Jump at the Sun, 2005.
   (CSK Winner)

The People Could Fly: The Picture Book by Virginia Hamilton. Knopf, 2004. (CSK Honor)

A Wreath for Emmett Till by Marilyn Nelson. Houghton Mifflin, 2005. (CSK Honor, Printz Honor)

Dark Sons

By Nikki Grimes
N.Y., Hyperion/Jump at the Sun, 2005
Grade: 9–12
Genre: Poetry
Core Democratic Value: Pursuit of Happiness
*All people can find happiness in their own way,
as long as they do not step on the rights of others.*

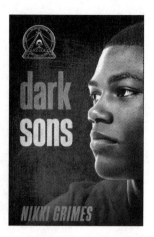

Content Perspective

Two firstborn sons—one from biblical times,
one contemporary—are heartbroken when their beloved fathers shift
their devotion to second son born by a second mother. The parallel
stories of Ishmael and Sam told alternately reveal the deep anger and
hurt they each feel from their father's betrayals. Nikki Grimes's powerful novel, written in free verse, traces the journey of both young men
toward forgiveness for their earthly fathers through the guidance of the
Father they "could count on."

Discussion Openers

Students should provide examples of text and/or illustrations to support
their responses.

- Identify three examples of a father's love in the lives of both Ishmael
  and Sam.
- Discuss evidence that Ishmael and Sam are ready to step up to the
  responsibilities created by their father's abandonment.
- Discuss the roles that friends, peers, and the half brother played in
  helping or hindering Sam's and Ishmael's ability to cope with their
  situations.
- Using an online biblical commentary, locate the book in the Bible
  where the character Ishmael can be found. Compare and contrast
  the story of Ishmael with the characters in *Dark Sons*.
- Discuss the potential of a future relationship between Ishmael,
  Sam, and their stepbrother.

Beyond the Book

- Start a forgiveness journal in which you write about a person in your life who has hurt you, and how you might go about forgiving him or her.
- Find two of the following locations: Egypt, Niger, Mamre, Chaldea, Gerar, Canaan. Compare their geographical similarities and differences.
- Using the online Bible commentary, locate the book in the Bible where the character Ishmael can be found. Retell his story.
- Write a letter of forgiveness to someone who has hurt you.
- Who was Ishmael's mother? Research information about her and write a brief summary of her life.

Books for Further Discussions

The Creation by James Weldon Johnson. Holiday House, 1994.
   (CSK Winner)

The First Part Last by Angela Johnson. Simon & Schuster, 2003.
   (CSK Winner, Printz Winner)

The Way a Door Closes by Hope Anita Smith, illus. by Shane W. Evans.
   Henry Holt, 2003. (CSK–John Steptoe Winner)

The First Part Last

By Angela Johnson
N.Y., Simon & Schuster, 2003
Grade: 8–12
Genre: Realistic Fiction
Core Democrat Value: Pursuit of Happiness
People have the right to pursue happiness in their own way, as long as they do not infringe upon the rights of others.

Content Perspective

The First Part Last is the story of sixteen-year-old Bobby, urban New Yorker, high school senior, and custodial father of his newborn daughter, Feather. Short chapters chronicle Bobby's life, alternating between now and then. Bobby's struggles with the real-life challenges of fatherhood in the absence of Nia, the baby's mother, is an alternate perspective on the traditional baby-momma/baby-daddy plot.

Discussion Openers

Students should provide examples of text and/or illustrations to support their responses.

- How would your life change if you suddenly became a teenage parent?
- Bobby's mother loves her son and her new grandbaby, but she is firm in her resolve not to take over Bobby's parenting duties. Why?
- How important is it to the story that Bobby has running buddies?
- If you are a boy, do you believe you could parent a newborn child as Bobby does in the story? If you are a girl, which do you believe would be best: to agree to having the teen father care for your child, or to give it up for adoption?
- Why did Bobby leave New York and move with Feather to Ohio?

Beyond the Book

- Rewrite the title for Angela Johnson's book. Defend your choice.
- Create an outline for a sequel to *The First Part Last* as a television show.
- Collect statistics on the number of teenage parents in your community.
- Collect statistics on the number of teenage parents who put their babies up for adoption.
- Investigate the resources available to pregnant teens in your community and post them in your school.

Books for Further Discussions

Chill Wind by Janet McDonald. Farrar, Straus and Giroux, 2002. (CSK–John Steptoe Winner)

November Blues by Sharon Draper. Atheneum, 2007. (CSK Honor)

Somewhere in the Darkness by Walter Dean Myers. Scholastic, 1992. (CSK Honor, Newbery Honor)

The Way a Door Closes by Hope Anita Smith, illus. by Shane W. Evans. Henry Holt, 2003. (CSK–John Steptoe Winner)

Who Am I Without Him? Short Stories About Girls and the Boys in Their Lives

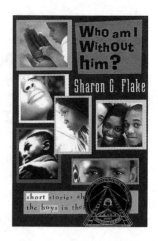

By Sharon G. Flake

N.Y., Hyperion/Jump at the Sun, 2004

Grade: 9–12

Genre: Realistic Fiction

Core Democratic Value: Pursuit of Happiness
It is the right of citizens in the United States to pursue happiness in their own way, as long as they do not infringe on the rights of others.

Content Perspective

This collection of stories about urban youth and their relationships speaks to both the male and female's sense of self. Sharon Flake's ear for language and realistic dialogue invites the reader to identify with the characters in each story as they experience painful truths about love, respect, and the realities of decisions made in haste. The letter from an absentee father to his daughter provides the reader with instinctive survival skills needed to navigate a typical teenage world.

Discussion Openers

Students should provide examples of text and/or illustrations to support their responses.

- Select three stories from the book *Who Am I Without Him? Short Stories About Girls and the Boys in Their Lives* and create a new title for each.
- Discuss the evidence that supports the characterization of Mookie as a favored son.
- Reread the last chapter, "A Letter to My Daughter." Pick three stories and assign one of the father's advisory notes to the girl in each story.

- Who is the bully in the story "The Ugly One"? How did Asia choose to resolve the situation? What would you have done differently?
- What messages do the stories in the book deliver about how to be a man?

Beyond the Book

- Prepare an interview questionnaire for classmates of the opposite sex regarding their point of view on dating.
- Define respectful behaviors as you know them. Include respect for peers, parents, adult family members, and respect for other adults, including strangers.
- Appearance, beauty, and looks are a frequent theme in stories about teens. Select a teen magazine and evaluate the depictions of teens.
- Identify three positive influences available to teens in your community.
- Create a dictionary of teenspeak words and phrases.

Books for Further Discussions

Jazmin's Notebook by Nikki Grimes. Dial, 1998. (CSK Honor)

The Young Landlords by Walter Dean Myers. Puffin, 1979. (CSK Winner)

The Battle of Jericho by Sharon M. Draper. Atheneum, 2003. (CSK Honor)

The Tequila Worm by Viola Canales. Wendy Lamb, 2005. (Pura Belpre Winner)

A Wreath for Emmett Till

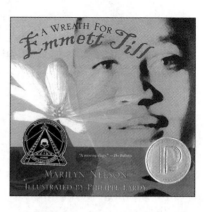

By Marilyn Nelson
N.Y., Houghton Mifflin, 2005
Grade: 9–12
Genre: Biography/Poetry
Core Democratic Value: Life
The individual's right to live should be considered inviolable.

Content Perspective

Marilyn Nelson has memorialized the life of Emmett Till in a heroic crown of beautiful heart-wrenching sonnets. Till was an innocent fourteen-year-old whose stuttering whistle, misinterpreted as being directed at a white woman, led to his brutal beating and drowning death. His story is one of many incidents that sparked the civil rights movement.

Discussion Openers

Students should provide examples of text and/or illustrations to support their responses.

- Reread "Pierced by the Screams of a Shortened Childhood." Think about the legal and social practices in place that would not allow this to happen today.
- Select the most hopeful sonnet and create an illustration that reflects your choice.
- Describe the impact of the decision by Emmett Till's mother to allow a photograph of Emmett's body to be published.
- Make a list of vocabulary words used by author Marilyn Nelson that are unfamiliar to you. Research their definitions.
- What strategies did Emmett learn to use to counteract his stuttering in a stressful situation? How might these strategies have served him had he been allowed to live?

Beyond the Book

- Describe Nelson's use of a "heroic crown of sonnets." Contrast this particular style with those of other writers (e.g., Carole Boston Weatherford's *Becoming Billie Holiday*).
- Research the laws relating specifically to blacks that pertained to their rights and restrictions prior to the civil rights movement.
- Are there programs or practices in place today that encourage civility between people of different backgrounds, cultures, or ethnicities?
- Interview a grandparent or other family member about his or her recollections of the Emmett Till saga and other events leading to the civil rights movement.
- Use traditional black media (e.g., *Ebony*, *Jet*, *Chicago Defender*, *Amsterdam News*) to research the life and death of Emmett Till. Compare and contrast these perspectives with information you find in the *New York Times* or your local newspaper.

Books for Further Discussions

Copper Sun by Sharon Draper. Atheneum, 2006. (CSK Winner)

Dark Sons by Nikki Grimes. Hyperion/Jump at the Sun, 2005. (CSK Honor)

Day of Tears by Julius Lester. Hyperion/Jump at the Sun, 2005. (CSK Winner)

About the Authors

Adelaide Poniatowski Phelps has a master's degree in library and information science from Wayne State University in Detroit and a second master's degree in English literature from Oakland University in Rochester, Michigan. She is the recently retired coordinator of the Educational Resources Lab in the School of Education and Human Services at Oakland University and a former lecturer in children's literature for the reading department there. She is a member of the Coretta Scott King Book Awards Committee and served two terms (2007–2008) on the awards jury. In addition, she was a reviewer for the journal *Multicultural Review;* a contributing reviewer for the fourth edition of *The Coretta Scott King Awards 1970–2009* book, edited by Henrietta M. Smith; a contributing author for the article (2008), "Weaving the Threads of Diversity: A School of Education's Reflection on Current Practices" in the journal *Issues in Education: Preschool through Graduate School* 1(1): 43–50; and coauthor of the chapter, "Information and Instruction Services" in *A Guide to the Management of Curriculum Materials Centers for the 21st Century: The Promise and the Challenge* (2001), edited by Jo Ann Carr and prepared by the Ad Hoc Management of Curriculum Materials Committee, Education and Behavioral Sciences Section, Association of College and Research Libraries.

Carole J. McCollough is a retired associate professor and dean of the Library and Information Science program at Wayne State University. She is currently an auxiliary faculty, trainer, and curriculum committee member for the Children's Defense Fund. In this capacity, Carole conducts workshops for college interns training to run summer literacy (Freedom School) programs. In addition to serving as chair of the CSK Book Award Committee, she served one term on the CSK Book Award jury and two terms as chair. She was a reviewer for the *Multicultural Literature Review Journal* and a contributing reviewer to *The Coretta Scott King Awards 1970–2009* first, second, third, and fourth editions, published by ALA. Her undergraduate degree and teaching certificate are from Eastern Michigan University. Her master's degree and PhD in library and information science are both from the University of Michigan in Ann Arbor. She currently serves on two library boards: Southfield Public Library, Southfield, Michigan, and the Langston Hughes Library, Clinton, Tennessee.

Index